W9-BUE-491

# Best Sermons 1925

Edited with Introduction and Biographical Notes by

Joseph Fort Newton
(D.D., Litt.D.)
Memorial Church of St. Paul, Philadelphia; Late of Church of the Divine Paternity, New York
Author of "Some Living Masters of the Pulpit," "Preaching in London," "Preaching in New York," "The Sword of the Spirit," etc.

New York
Harcourt, Brace and Company

PRINTED IN THE U. S. A. BY
QUINN & BODEN COMPANY, INC.
RAHWAY, N. J.

# IN THE VESTRY

*For the pulpit is ever this earth's foremost part; all the rest comes in its rear; the pulpit leads the world. From thence it is that the storm of God's quick wrath is first descried, and the bow must bear the earliest brunt. From thence it is that the God of breezes fair or foul is first invoked for favorable winds. Yes, the world's a ship on its passage out, and not a voyage complete; and the pulpit is its prow.*

—Herman Melville, *Moby Dick.*

The cordial reception with which the first volume of Best Sermons was greeted is most encouraging, as showing the interest in preaching when it is the voice of a warm, spiritual, consecrated manhood, in which art and insight are joined, speaking the language of faith without regard to sect. In the present volume a larger number of communions are represented, and the editor rejoices in the coöperation of both the Jewish and the Catholic pulpits, not alone for the high quality of the sermons contributed, but also to make plain that in our pulpit symphony all voices are welcome: only exclusiveness is excluded.

The labor of preparing such a volume is prodigious, but it is extraordinarily interesting, and it suggests many reflections. Our generation, if not actually suffering from suppressed religion, at least has an intense, eager, wistful longing for a more satisfying sense of spiritual reality; a desire for spiritual support from a source hid in spiritual mystery, as a reservoir of motive, as a spring of health, as a secret of inner power, as a dynamic of social idealism. There has never been so vast a force of incipient spiritual activity, to be influenced and directed for good or ill, as there is today. What an opportunity for the pilot-voice at the prow of our Ship of the Spirit, sailing in new and strange waters; a voice free alike from panics of faith and dogmatic depressives, yet true to those bosom-mysteries out of which are the issues of life.

Yet there is a widespread impression that the pulpit has lost its bearings, and that from its message the note of authority and the thrill of momentousness have died out, leaving the instinct of evangelic persuasion in abeyance. In so far as this impression is justified—and one does miss in the preaching of today the urgency of appeal, as of a herald telling tidings of vast moment, as well as a certain quality of unction so notable in former times—it is due alike to pulpit and people, and to the conditions under which they live. The pulpit has fallen, not upon evil days, but upon other days. The voices of the age call men away from the inner life; psychology seeks to dissolve it into mist and dream; and we are almost imperceptibly led to neglect its laws and disciplines. Our life is cluttered with things external; our literature gives us little more than passing thoughts of eternal realities. Science has unveiled a universe so vast that every man by himself is a bit lonely in it, and what we need—pulpit and people alike—is to rediscover the still greater heights and depths of the Kingdom of Heaven which is within.

Yet the conditions of life in our age, especially in our cities, are a challenge to those who would interpret the things of the spirit. Everything is so speeded up, so crowded, so smitten with the fever of haste as to make meditation and worship almost lost arts. Flashlight glimpses and spotlight thinking make a kind of mind so jumpy and scrappy and scattered that a large part of the public lacks the mental concentration, if not the capacity, to follow sustained thought; and that state of fact creates a changed atmosphere for preaching. For one thing, it makes expository preaching, so fruitful in other days, well-nigh impossible, in America at least. The reading of hundreds of sermons, in order to make this selection, did not reveal a single example of that type of preaching. Such preaching must of necessity assume some knowledge of the Bible, in respect to which most of our hearers are almost illiterate, and half proud of the fact, counting it a little gray sin to be coddled, lest they be deemed too pious.

Great and deep themes can hardly be dealt with when the demand is that everything be "brief, breezy, snappy, something doing every minute." It is interesting to study the popular preacher of today, in contrast with Beecher, Brooks, and Joseph Parker, who swayed men as the winds sway the clouds. The preacher of today must win by other arts, chiefly by "artistic repetition"—saying one thing many times and in many ways—in obedience to the wisdom of *Alice in Wonderland,* where it is said: "What I tell you three times is true." In short, we have a new keyboard upon which to play the everlasting music; and the fingers of our sermons often grope blindly over its hidden keys. Yet when we do strike the great chords, in a manner not unworthy of the melodies they invoke, the hearts of men respond with a startled and wistful joy.

In these despites we have a great pulpit today, as this volume bears witness, in many keys and tones eloquent in behalf of the spiritual life in a hurrying time. The prophet of today, as in all the days agone, must learn to live where insight is pure and piercing, where moral earnestness rises into passion, and where the ancient oracle of God repeats its truth to the heart. He must look upon life with purified and exalted vision; his vision must become utterance; and his utterance must commend itself by the integrity of his intellect and his life. No servers of tables, no fellow of those strange sons of privilege who think earth is heaven, much less a boon companion of that portion of society whose ears are so stuffed with selfishness that they cannot hear the cry of those for whom civilization is often only exclusion from the life proper to human beings, can minister to the need of our day. The preacher must live with the people if he is to know their problems, and he must live with God if he is ever to solve them.

Evermore we who minister the things of the spirit must live the innermost life of the spirit, where God makes character, and where souls renew their being in Him. From that sphere in which all higher living originates and from which it is guided and sustained, we must do our work, keeping close to the poetry and piety of the ages; it is our native air. Who shall say that for the future new births in this holy line of descent are impossible; that the Life of the Spirit has expended itself and may not achieve to new and more perfect forms; that the Eternal Evangel may not be preached to suffering and despairing men, proclaiming in words all may hear and understand the miracle of the healing of the nations, the coming of an abiding peace, and the realization of God by the practice of the Brotherhood of Man!

Like the men in *Moby Dick* who listened to Father Mapple, we too are sailors, afloat but not adrift, upon the waters that flow about the universe, swept by Winds of the Spirit which blow where they list, but do not run at random. We go, trusting, God willing, that good seamanship and a wise Pilot shall win to some undiscovered shore of human good. What though some ancient landmarks may fade from view:

other and more splendid guiding peaks will rise to sight. Always the quest is for the liberty of faith, for the fraternity of service, for the redemption of man in a Beloved Community—and the voyaging is not in vain.

JOSEPH FORT NEWTON.

Memorial Church of St. Paul,
Overbrook, Philadelphia.

*Publisher's Note*

This volume represents the church year 1924-1925: from annual conference to annual conference.

# CONTENTS

# Contents

# KEEPING THE FAITH

Bishop Slattery is a son of the Rectory, born in Pittsburgh in 1867; educated at Harvard and at the Episcopal Theological School, Cambridge; and ordained a priest in 1895. For two years master of Groton School; dean of Faribault Cathedral; rector of Christ Church, Springfield; in 1910 he came to historic Grace Church, New York City, where he spent twelve happy and notable years. Since 1922 he has been Bishop Coadjutor of Massachusetts, as well as General Chairman of the Church Congress of the United States.

As an author he is prolific, but never prolix, uniting literary grace with spiritual insight, alike in poetry and prose, in sermon and essay. He has written so many biographies of famous churchmen as almost to entitle him to be called a Plutarch of the Rectory—the last being a sketch of the late William Austin Smith, editor of *The Churchman*. Among books too many to name, dealing with almost every phase of the spiritual life, it is not easy to select; but some of us love best *The Gift of Immortality,* and his essays on Prayer, *Why Men Pray, How to Pray,* and *A Study of the Lord's Prayer*—not forgetting a tiny book of prayers, worth its weight in gold.

The sermon on Keeping the Faith is timely, in the midst of angry agitations in the churches, and is itself an example of the faith which it expounds—a faith able to live and triumph amid vast and unimagined developments of thought and life, making the new learning of science an instrument, not an enemy, as it has done with other advances of the human mind in ages agone. Withal it is so wise, so finely poised, so aglow with confident expectation, as befits those who would follow One who "made as though He would have gone further" on a sacramental eventide.

# KEEPING THE FAITH

CHARLES LEWIS SLATTERY, D.D.
BISHOP COADJUTOR OF MASSACHUSETTS, BOSTON

*I have kept the faith.* II Timothy 4: 7.

What does it really mean to keep the faith? How shall we use the great Christian confidence which we have received from our fathers, that to the people who shall take our places we may pass it on with vigor and enthusiasm?

Our thoughts go back to a leader of the first century who said in a proud humility that he had kept the faith. It has been said that Christ came with His divine message and St. Paul was the perfect response. Christ lived in an obscure corner of the world of His day, trusting those who loved Him to carry His power not only into the world of that time, but into the world of all time. St. Paul did not know Christ in the days of the Lord's earthly ministry. He received, through the revelation of Christ in other men's lives and through the direct revelation in his own life, the outstanding facts and teachings of the Master. Before he finished his course he had made Christ so known to the world that the world could never forget Him. He had so kept that which had been given him that it lived for the future because it had passed through his loyal experience.

We have a glimpse in such a life of what it is to keep the faith. It is not a talent folded up in a napkin and buried in the earth, to be dug up by others as a lifeless curiosity. It is a breathing, pulsating thing: growing, absorbing out of its neighborhood new and vivid expression, making itself intelligible and vital for each new age. It is not a lazy, comfortable task, this keeping of the faith. It abounds in risk; it requires devotion; it needs an acute mind; above all it must have a love which is willing to count all things lost if Christ be not shown supreme.

Let me therefore briefly sum up the way in which this man of the first century kept the faith, and then let me try to apply it to ourselves.

First, St. Paul filled the faith of his fathers with the divine life of his own day. His countrymen treated him as a traitor, believing that he was destroying that ancient gift from on high. Not only did St. Paul protest that he was bringing all the revelation which God had made to Israel, to its necessary completion in Christ, but subsequent history was to show that a Christian world had kept aglow in men's hearts the sublime message of the Old Testament prophets. Christ's promise had indeed been kept: He had not destroyed, but fulfilled.

Secondly, the Apostle Paul, while profoundly convinced of the truth which he taught, held that whole body of truth to be so great a thing that he could not pretend to reduce it all to definition and demonstration. In the highest utterance[1] of his life, he said: "Now we see through a glass darkly; but then face to face: now I know in part; but then shall I know even as also I am known." He opposed those who believed themselves the appointed guardians of the truth, and would fit all God's revelation into narrow terms—the legalists who opposed the freedom of the Gospel, the Simon Peters who questioned the rights of Gentile Christians, the men who spoke with tongues and pitied the saner members of the flock. He was willing to wait for fuller revelation in the world to come.

Thirdly, St. Paul appealed to a living experience. He did not scorn records and traditions; he revered and used them. But there was one test above all else, absolutely essential. He dared to say, "To me, to live is Christ." Christ was a present reality. No man could so keep the faith as to pass it on who was not aware of that living Presence.

Thus we find the framework for our study this morning of the way in which we may keep the faith. Let us examine it in terms of our own living.

[1] I Cor. 13.

## Charles Lewis Slattery, D.D.

I

The first principle of keeping the faith is to allow the divine revelation of our own day to breathe through the faith which has come down to us; or, if you wish to reverse the process, to let the faith which has come down to us breathe through the divine revelation in our own time. The God who spoke in Jesus of Nazareth is the God who is a Living Voice in this very year. The Voice is acknowledged when the accents are heard in the hearts of living generations.

As you glance back through the centuries you see that the ages of increased knowledge of our Lord have come through the penetration of His Spirit into the spirit of the times. Greek thought which was the expression of the civilized world caught up the Christian message and in the early General Councils interpreted Christ in Greek terms for the fourth and fifth centuries. In medieval and later art the Child of Bethlehem was throned in His mother's arms; but both Child and mother were not from the Palestine of the first century, they were from the country and time of the reverent painter. Christ had come into that country and that age, and spoke through its common life. The English language came to its richness in the days of Shakespeare; so the story of Christ fused itself through that translucent medium, and we have the Gospels not only according to the four Evangelists, but, in addition, according to the glowing utterance of a great age.

Now we are in an age of scientific discovery. It is an age tingling with the poetry of a vast world revealed by telescope and microscope and the genius of men. This age too belongs to Christ. The God who is revealed through modern geology and astronomy and biology and chemistry is the Father of our Lord Jesus Christ.

All the past interpretations are good and inspiring. But they are not so inspiring for us as the interpretation of Christ in our own time. We may not keep the faith by any easy lip-service, by any parrot-like repetition of what previous ages have said about Him. We must bring whatever the world is telling us now about God and mingle it with the pristine message of the Gospel itself. Christ must live in the terms of the experience of our own day. If He so lives, we shall not need to insist on words valid for the fourth or the tenth or the seventeenth century. He will be clothed with the majesty of this very year and its revelation. He will be a thrilling reality. He will absorb all past tokens and symbols in the white light which comes from a living Presence. Men will not question doctrines and creeds of the past, because they have all that these give, and then much more. They will see the Saviour in His own wondrous world of today.

May we believe in Christ so thoroughly that we

may see Him in the most searching truth of the modern world, and thereby show Him to our time that this time may believe in Him! So we shall have kept the faith.

## II

How, in the second place, shall we exalt our Lord in the faith of our time? Think again of the ringing words: "Now we see through a glass darkly . . . now I know in part." There are two classes of men who tend to deny the faith in Christ. One class comes forward with meticulous criticism of this detail and that, and explains that Christ could not have said this or could not have done that. They sharply define the region of the possible. The other class which tends to deny Christ, piles up the details about our Lord's Character and Person, and defines with acid sharpness every one of them. Neither class is willing to say, "Now we see through a glass darkly . . . now I know in part." Both classes brazenly assert that everything is forever defined.

I do not pour scorn on these methods. All I am concerned to do is to proclaim that such people do not keep the faith in the hearts of their neighbors. If men could only kneel in true reverence before the Lord Christ, if only they could feel the radiance that shines from His face, if only they could suspect the mystery of His power, if only they could be warned that for love's sake He may possibly forbear to use that power, then they would enter the baffling joy of accepting Him without attempting too carefully to describe Him. If prompted to tell what they see and feel and know at such a moment, they would always say, "This I know in part."

The clearer revelation need not all be withheld till this world passes. Some of it may come in time. One illustration may help. A little after the middle of the last century a strife arose in the Church about Baptismal Regeneration. One group said that for infants unconscious of the baptism which they were receiving it were pure magic to talk of such a change. Another group defined exactly what the change was, and read out of the Church any who disagreed. Fifty years have gone, and I think it would now be impossible to revive the controversy. Men's convictions are not less vigorous, but their ideas have enlarged. We now see the infant, not as an individual distinct from the rest of humanity, but as an inseparable part of humanity. He is partly the love of his mother, the care of his father, the friendship of his parents' friends, the expectancy of older brothers or sisters, the interest of teachers who are to come. All these have already entered into his life or shall enter it a little later. He cannot be defined without them. They are as much part of him as his hands and his feet. If any of these bring him to baptism, it is part of himself which brings him. He, in them, takes responsibility. He, through them, receives a new birth. Baptismal regeneration begins to take on the meaning of our modern language. We do not know all it means. But it does mean something to us, more possibly than it has meant to any generation before.

Would it not be wise if we could so treat every truth which has been cherished in the past, and which has ceased perhaps to have much meaning for a good many people of the time in which we chance to live? There is the clause in the Creed which refers to the manner of our Lord's entrance into human life. There is a tendency to define what that means or cannot mean. I cannot believe that either way the faith in Christ is kept for our time. Can we not say, "Now see we through a glass darkly, . . . now I know in part"? This is not cowardice, but reverence. Where all words and accounts are inadequate, why not leave so sacred a record in trust? It has meant much to the past. It surely will mean new light upon the Saviour's life in the future. If you force a meaning which does not really command your intelligent assent, you are not reverencing Christ, but dishonoring the Master of all Truth, who He is. If you deny any possible meaning, you are diminishing the glory of the mystery which shines always over Him. If you humbly and confidently say, "Now we see through a glass darkly . . . now I know in part," you can afford to wait. You shall know the truth and the truth shall make you free. It will never be less than you dared to think: it will always be more.

Let us who long to make known the living Christ, be modest in placing limits in so transcendent a Presence. Let us worship and love and serve Him. Let us tell what we can, but before we limit and define Him, let us wait till He deigns to tell us all. So, once more, we shall keep the faith.

## III

Let us pass now to the final stage by which we may truly keep the faith. The words echo down the centuries, "I live, yet not I; but Christ liveth in me." There is the real keeping of the faith, the life of Christ manifest in His own among each generation.

One or two illustrations I give you. The author of the fourth Gospel has a power over us which exceeds the authority of the rest of the New Testament writings. He does not give so literal a record of our Lord's words and deeds as the writers of the other Gospels. But in such passages as the fourteenth chapter, and in the discourses on the Good Shepherd and the Vine, he brings us into the Presence of the Lord. Why? Because the fourth Gospel is the record of Christ as Christ has made Himself known to a great and loving Mystic at the end of the first century. In the author we see Christ shining through.

Centuries passed. Francis of Assisi started out upon his singular career. We do not understand all the phenomena of his devoted life, such as the reputed nail-prints in the feet and hands. But we do know that St. Francis was a Christ-filled man. Christ was made known in a new and vivid way because men saw Him in the face and words and deeds of the simple man of Assisi.

Think of the last century. Charles Lamb was not, we think, on the same level with St. Francis, yet, as we read his life, we think that he too caught in his unselfish, noble devotion, the life of the one Master of us all. No man, it seems, could know Charles Lamb without being drawn to Christ.

Thackeray created a character called Colonel Newcome. He is a type of honorable, Christ-filled life—a portrait on a large scale, much more than a biography, but quite as true as a biography. No one can know Colonel Newcome without feeling Christ coming to him in terms of nineteenth century experience.

We read the life of Louis Pasteur, one of the very greatest scientists of all time. We see him at home; in his laboratory; on his errands to save life—and we perceive Christ shining through him. He reveals in nineteenth century science the Christ of all the ages.

The company of such Christ-filled people no man can number. They are of all times and of all lands. I doubt not there are many in this church today. In other ways you may keep the faith, but this is the way above all others.

Not long ago I heard this story in a little village church in France. A new pastor had come to the village, and called at a certain cottage. When the husband came home from his work, the wife said, "The new pastor called today." "What did he say?" asked the man. "Oh," she answered, "he asked, 'Does Christ live here?' and I didn't know what to say." The man's face flushed: "Why didn't you tell him that we were respectable people," he said. "Well," she answered, "I might have said that: only that isn't what he asked me." "Then why," pursued her husband, "didn't you tell him that we said our prayers and read our Bibles?" The wife replied, "But he didn't ask me that." The man grew more vexed: "Why," he continued, "didn't you say that we were always at church?" The poor woman broke down: "He didn't ask that either: he asked only, 'Does Christ live here?' " This man and woman pondered for many days what the grave pastor meant by his question. Little by little their lives were changed. Little by little they grew to expect Christ —not dead, but gloriously alive. And some way, they knew not how, through great love, and through a willingness to be surprised by the mystery of His radiance, they knew Him. He did indeed live there.

O men and women, let Christ into your individual lives. Surrender to Him absolutely and entirely. Grant to Him your lips that He may speak; grant to Him your hands that He may serve; grant to Him your feet that He may go to all who need friendship and care; grant to Him your hearts that they may overflow with His pity and His love. Be lost to yourselves that He, in you, may be found for the saving of this generation. You will not know that He is using you. That He has used you, and shall use you forever, is part of the amazing glory which shall be revealed.

How silently, how silently,
  The wondrous gift is given!
So God imparts to human hearts
  The blessings of His heaven.
No ear may hear His coming,
  But in this world of sin,
Where meek souls will receive Him, still
  The dear Christ enters in.

# THE GREAT HUNGER

Rabbi Blau is a native of Hungary who came to America at the age of twenty-four, entering the University of Cincinnati, from which he was graduated in 1908. Ordained a rabbi the same year, at the Hebrew Union College, he continued his studies at Columbia University until 1909, when he began his ministry in Brooklyn. Since 1912 he has served congregations in Manhattan, and at present is rabbi of Peni-El Temple, 147th Street and Broadway.

Aside from his work as a preacher, in which he is devoted to the high ideal and tradition of the pulpit, as over against the popular devices now in vogue, he is a frequent contributor to periodical literature, both Jewish and general. His article entitled "My Uncertain God," in a recent issue of the *Menorah Journal,* deserved a wide reading, as did his striking essay in the *Atlantic Monthly.* He has also written a number of scholarly treatises on questions of Jewish jurisprudence and studies of various aspects of Jewish mysticism.

During the present year Rabbi Blau took all of us captive with a remarkable book entitled *The Wonder of Life,* which Israel Zangwill described as "the most original book about religion, the most daring and paradoxical, ever written by an American Rabbi, or, for the matter of that, by any American ecclesiastic." It is neither sermons nor essays, but a series of visions such as Emerson might have written had he been born in Judea, or a Jewish seer might give us had he grown up in New England.

The following sermon, if less epigrammatic than the book—as a sermon should be—reveals much of the same artistry of insight, imagery, and rhythm; and it must surely find response in those who feel the pathos and passion and prophecy of the modern yearning for spiritual reality.

## THE GREAT HUNGER

RABBI JOEL BLAU

PENI-EL TEMPLE, NEW YORK CITY

*Behold, the days come, saith the Lord God, that I will send a famine in the land, not a famine of bread, nor a thirst for water, but of hearing the words of the Lord. . . . They shall run to and fro to seek the word of the Lord, and shall not find it.* Amos 8: 11, 12.

### I

There is a stir of something strange moving through the world today, and we all feel it. There is a mighty wind blowing through space, and the treetops are agitated. The very air we breathe is tremulous and tense, as if with tidings of a new birth. The feet of the messenger are again on the mountains: we hear the sound of advancing steps, but we do not know whither they are tending. A Something vague, a Namelessness without shape or outline, has laid its hand upon us; and, though we know it not very clearly, we are aware of a guidance toward uncharted regions of human experience, of a Finger pointing to some fair Promised Land far off.

One thing only in all this agitation of our time stands out with unmistakable definiteness. Men and women are restless, but not with the restlessness of those who have lost their path and given up in despair, rather with the hopeful questings of those who are seeking a way and are sure to find it. Theirs is a passionate groping, but their very darkness is as light. Theirs is a search after newer and truer values, a purposeful adventure of the spirit. These men and women are in the grip of a Great Hunger which, like all great hungers, feeds on itself, growing on what it gets, growing still more on what it fails to get. But they cannot ever be daunted in their quest: for they know, if they know aught, that the time of the Great Fulfillment cannot be put off. The very hunger which stalks abroad among the people everywhere is in itself a presage of that fulfillment, a sure token of the prophetic times in which we live: for has the coming of this Great Hunger not been foretold by Amos ages ago? Listen:

> Behold, the days come, saith the Lord God, that I will send a famine in the land, not a famine of bread, nor a thirst for water, but of hearing the words of the Lord. And they shall wander from sea to sea and from the north even to the east, they shall run to and fro to seek the word of the Lord, and shall not find it.

Can you fancy a more graphic description of the very body and spirit of our age? Can you imagine a more vivid limning of the Great Hunger of the spirit? Ah, he, the prophet of God, has known the pangs of this hunger; he has known the labor and the agony of it: the tossing from sea to sea, the braving of the dangers of the deep (the depths of the soul hold graver perils than the abysses of the ocean), the wandering through the dark north-country toward the light-flooded east, is no foreign experience to him. But if he has known the gloom of the quest, he has also learnt its glories; if his was the weariness of running to and fro, his also was the blessedness of finding.

This last blessedness he denies the people he addresses. But this last blessedness we should not deny our own generation. Amos knew his time, and we know ours. The Great Hunger is upon us, yet we feel that what we seek we shall find—the word of God to our own time and generation.

## II

We are strangely hungry beings—hungry and haunted. Our hungers are many, our satisfactions few. But even if we could multiply the satisfaction, we should nevertheless reach out after that which haunts us continually. For it is not immediate satisfactions we crave: at least not the best of us. The immediate does not appeal to us: we rebel against the urgency and tyranny of the moment. Our lives we know possess a fringe quality, and it is this invisible fringe of our existence, stretching away into infinitude, and not the crude visible material contents of our being, that arouses in us the most passionate desire, the most tormenting thirst. We would know it, this elusive fringe of our life, we would make it real to ourselves; we would grasp the far-flung affinities it bears with a Vaster Life ever near yet ever far; we would behold this aura of loves and values, of admirations and remote idealisms, which enhaloes us: touching us very nearly, yet never becoming entirely part of our curiously mixed temper, and withal radiating off into a realm of mystery where its true origin seems to be. Oh, we are like the Midnight Sun, which appears as the crown worn by the Queen of the Night up in the North, whose center is darkness and which flashes into the sable air to be lost in the far spaces. Shall we who wear this luminous crown never know its nature, never really make ourselves worthy of it?

We are strangely hungry beings, but our very worth depends upon the number and nature of our hungers. We are capable of low hungers, such as give scarce an intimation of the noble fringe quality of human life. We are capable also of low satisfactions, such as dim the glory of the spirit. Some physicists maintain that everybody carries about him a surrounding aura or atmosphere, and that this airy envelope of the body may be seen with appropriate instruments; it is also maintained that this insubstantial sheath changes its color with the condition of the person and may be studied for the diagnosis of disease. So one fancies that some of our cravings and their unhallowed gratification must mar our outward semblance. Certain it is that some men and women manifestly carry about them as if a garment of light, while others are wrapped in darkness, so that as soon as they enter a room we know whether they are on the side of the angels or no. But when we analyze our first impressions, and try to account for the pleasant or unpleasant impact of an alien personality upon our own, we usually find that the effect, for better or worse, emanates from the fringe: from the subtle quality which the alien life communicates to us. But this quality, on further analysis, is found to be the fruit of tastes cultivated and followed, of the high or low level on which a person's hungers and enjoyments move. For we are what we seek. Our selections and our rejections determine our lives. Whatever we find, our own phantom self stares us in the face. Our desires and hungers are the measure of our soul. Mean hungers flow out of mean lives. Great hungers spring from great lives.

We are strangely hungry beings, and therefore our hungers are many and great. We hunger for Beauty. We chase after this magic deer, which ever eludes us and often leads us astray into thick, poison-reeking jungles. But we chase after it, being ever spurred onward by the fitful glimpses it allows us of its fair body and fairer spirit, for we recognize in it one of the attributes of the Divine manifested in harmony of color, of line, and of sound. Through this obtuse and inchoate dust which we tread, through this obtuse and inchoate dust which we are, this fair young spirit of Beauty breaks, leaping from form to form and carrying with it a free glad breath as if from the world's first youth; and, although we know not its sheer essence, there are moments when we should like to believe that it is the redeeming angel of all life, sent here into this vale of our tears and fears to reconcile us to all the terror and tragedy of our perishing lives: for, say we, a world which can be so surpassing fair is a world worth living in and dying in: aye, is a world worth dying *into*. So potent is the spell of Beauty upon us that, on occasion, when purged of all impurities that by a strange fatality will cling to it, we feel in its presence a great, solemn thrill: we verily feel, as young Phidias must have felt in ancient Greece, the holiness of beauty.

Nevertheless, we know in our moments of deepest inseeing that this is not our Great, at least not our Greatest Hunger. For greater than the holiness of beauty is the beauty of holiness: loftier than the hills of Athens and Rome are the hills of Zion and Jerusalem—the mountains of God where the impatient feet of Judea's prophets were planted on days of great revelation, where among others Amos first raised the cry of the soul's insatiate hunger.

# The Great Hunger

We hunger for Truth, for Knowledge. In this world of many doubts, where paths cross and recross, where signposts covered with strange writing point in many and confusing directions, how we long for certainty! Certainty of knowledge that shall map out for us the whole of the universe, certainty of conduct that shall make our way sure before us. Our proximate ideal is sure-footedness—not a very high ideal, indeed, as it stifles the venturesome spirit; but none the less one in which many would like to rest, like a very lazy man who runs a half-mile in order to be able to let himself down on a bench he espies at a distance. If the world without as well as the world within could but be explored, until all things should be known, until the secrets hidden away in the heart of nature as in the heart of man should be revealed, man's quest would come to an end, and he might, so runs the confident prediction, master the universe and all that therein is and bend it to his purpose. Therefore have we of this modern day been searching high and low, in the heavens above and in the earth beneath, for new knowledge that shall give away the elusive secret which the Vast Wisdom abroad in the world seems to be persistently concealing from our hungry gaze.

We have lengthened our eye until it has seen farther than the ultimate star; we are examining vast nebulous stretches where worlds are cradled and nursed. We have delved into the caverns of the earth, in order to read the ancient runes engraven in the oldest Tablets of God whereby to reconstruct the story of life, as it danced in many-hued garments and in many evolutions of movement and grace on the greensward of this world. We have reached down into the depths of man's heart, trying to read his story in its recesses: we have hauled forth the underworld he bears in his bosom, trying to dispel his jungle fears and to banish the accumulated weaknesses of his stratified mind. What a wonderful task it was to expose, layer for layer, the making of the soul as it had been fashioned by Providence through man's many births and rebirths from ameba to Adam, from protozoan to poet and prophet! What wonder that in the face of these and similar achievements we are apt to feel that in Knowledge, as organized by science, we reach the high peak of human excellence, the last goal of human desire?

Nevertheless, we know in our moments of truest inseeing that this is not our Great, at least not our Greatest Hunger. For greater than the Known is the Unknown, greater than Knowledge is the Beyond-Ken. The little we have explored is overshadowed by the many darkling nooks and corners of this world which remain unexplored. And while we dare not assert that, either in the heart of the world or in the heart of man, these little unexplored and unexplained corners will forever remain so, yet, we know enough from our present explorations to suspect with certainty almost that the ultimate nature of things, probe as we may, will always remain unknown to us. Pursue the atom to its last hiding-place, and you will come upon a mysterious immaterial force which does not explain matter; pursue the least wayward wish of man to its furthest lair, and you come upon a primal longing, a hunger, which reaches out into a twilight region of the world's history where all being may have been one. Everywhere an untractable, irreducible, persisting fringe running over into the Beyond-Reason and the Beyond-Life. Knowledge, indeed, is one of the mighty passions of the soul, noble where it is purged of utility and mischief: but the Great Hunger of the soul is ever for the Unknown.

We hunger for Love, for companionship, for the happiness and the delight of freely chosen friendships. We yearn for the affection of father, for the tenderness of mother. Over the smile of a baby, our own or anybody's, we go into ecstasy: the chatter of baby lips, the patter of baby feet, seems to hold something divine. We cry out for the Eve who still stands in the Paradise of our dreams, flowerlike and inviolate, wreathed with fadeless light. We run to and fro to find the friend who in disinterested communion with ourselves might call forth the best in us and give us moments of purest bliss in which the blending of two lives would but serve to enhance each. But, much as these things mean to us, much as they fill our days with rich content, they still leave us empty, hungry, and unfulfilled. Our capacity for fellowship is so great that, after we have satisfied the claims of all these earthly loves, we send out the tendrils of our spirit into space to lay hold of the Very God, and to find in loving Him—*Him,* and not merely His manifestations; Him, as a felt Presence very near us—the last fulfillment of our being. No earthly love, no matter how pure, can fill this aching want for God. "When my father and mother forsake me," or when we forsake father and mother, too, in our search for infinite companionship, "then the Lord will take me up," for then we take up the Lord. We are soul, therefore our cry is for a Larger Soul. We are spirit, therefore we call unto the Great Spirit of the world. We are Personality, and therefore we would be drawn toward Personality. We have eternity locked in our breast, and therefore we can love the Eternal.

How abundant is our life! How it overflows from our lesser being into the infinite Being of the Father! Little is our heart and limited, yet into its littleness we would crowd the Fullness of God's life. With our short arms we would reach about the vastness of the universal life; hug all these riches to our perishing bosom; and proclaim with our dying breath that He is our Great Hunger—He alone—the Living God—our Greatest Hunger.

## III

What type of religion is it which might answer to this Great Hunger? which might be a worthy object for the passionate gropings of men and women today after a sustaining, tremendously vital faith?

It would seem that to define this religion would defeat its own purpose. For men and women, rightly, turn away from creedal statement, from hard and fast definitions which, like a closely woven network, would seek to catch truth in its meshes. Truth refuses to be caught in this fashion; and men and women, eager as perhaps never before in the world's history, will not play warden to help in the imprisonment of truth. They ask for the glad shout of freedom; not for the dismal rattling of chains and keys. They ask for the growth and grace of life; not for the stark frozen form of death. They have asked for these things so often, and asked in vain, that they are afraid to be fooled once more by any one who would pretend to set up a new creed, to formulate a new set of articles of belief. "New religions" in this sense are not wanted; in fact, one should be wary of enlarging the already too flourishing American industry—namely, the manufacture of new cults.

The religion men and women will accept is the religion which recognizes the principle of Growth. Truth must grow with the growth of human experience, and religion must register an unfeigned, unequivocal devotion to this growing body of human experience. Truth must be seen as greater than any statement of it; greater than any book, greater than any sage or saint. The truth which is alleged to be contained in unalterable form between the covers of a volume is not the work of God, it is the work only of the bookbinder. For the last revelation is not to be found on the last page preceding the last flyleaf: there is no last page, except as a necessity of the bookbinding trade. The last page, if written at all, is far off. Mankind will have to learn much, labor more, and suffer still more, before that last revelation can be had.

Truth is a flowing life. Truth is the spirit which dies into something else constantly reborn. Truth is God on the march, leaving, as He passes through the wilderness of worlds, His footprints behind: each of which is but a pointer to the next step, and to the next, perhaps endlessly. Truth is the gradual self-uncovery of God. The religion which is to answer to the Great Hunger is one that will bring to men and women this assurance of no-assurance, this affirmation of a large venturesome Spirit moving through timeless time, engaged in a vast experiment whose nature we can but dimly divine, but into which we must throw ourselves without mental reservation. It may be paradoxical, but is nevertheless true, that the kind of certainty which the dogmatists in religion would bring to the men and women of this age will leave them cold and unsympathetic, while the chaste intimations of the eternal life which the liberal religionist would bring to them, resembling so much the floating uncertainty of the summer cloud bathing in the beams of the sun, will hearten them and send them off on the world-path where God and man still walk together not in the cool of the day but in the heat and dust of the journey toward righteousness and truth.

And the religion which would answer to the Great Hunger would be one which, in the face of all uncertainty and in despite of all cosmic appearances to the contrary, would dare to make its affirmation of God's being so convincing as to banish all doubt. This is the world's crying need today: a tremendous reaffirmation of God as the Vast Life of the Universe and as the Near Friend and Companion of the heart of man. We stand over against the hollow emptiness of space: we wonder, is there anything that fills it? We face the mute skies: we wonder, is there any Life behind that curtained silence? Cosmic emptiness, cosmic silence, against which all our prayers and entreaties seem to be unavailing: we wonder, are these to be our lot? Is there no life out yonder that answers to our own? no eye that sees, no ear that hears, no heart that pities us and is akin to our own? Are we but parts of a gigantic soulless machine that somehow got itself wound up and is ready to pass over the fairest bodies and crush the finest aspirations, without ruth or regret, as it hulks in its blind brute way through all this world emptiness and all this world darkness? Or, rather, is this a living universe, with love beating at its miraculous heart, with mind ordering all its linked parts, with a vast congenial spirit impregnating it; a world where every particle of dust, gleaming in star, blowing in flower, or only lying opaquely underfoot, is alive and throbbing with a stupendous life; a world, where tragedy is the other side of comedy, even as terror is the other face of beauty, and where all cannot be known but where nevertheless some sublime plan ever unfolding itself before our eyes demands from us a loyalty truly cosmic—a loyalty passing the bounds of our loftiest private relationships—a loyalty which means the unconditional commitment of our whole life to a far-flung interest, whose barest fringe we may touch but whose full scope and extent we can at best but feebly glimpse?

This is the great question of our time; indeed, of all time. This is the question which haunts men and women in the work of the day and in the vision of the night. This is the question which carries a fear into heart of the stoutest, a fear underlying all other fears, overbrooding all pathetic human confidences: for if indeed it be true that we live in a dead universe, where we humans have to no intelligible purpose been shocked into living and into the agony of living, why should we live on, suffer on, carry on the hopeless human tradition? Ghastlier than any such conclusion concerning universal nature the human heart cannot conceive; and, therefore, it revolts from the inhumanity of a dead mechanical world whose God, if God it have, can but be the ironical God of Chance. And, therefore, the greatest achievement of the creative imagination—call it Faith, if you will—of man is to assert triumphantly, as Job did, "My redeemer liveth!" thus filling the emptiness of the world with the abundant life of God, the father of all life. And the religion of today, backed by all the resources of knowledge hitherto gained by man, must make this triumphant assertion in such a manner as to carry conviction to those who are under the spell of the Great Hunger.

And the religion which would answer to this Great Hunger must be one that would fill not only the hollows of the universal space, but also the hollows of the human heart. Who has not known the ghastly emptiness of the vacuous hours, when all seemed meaningless and without value, when our whole life seemed to be washed bare of all color and all warmth and all worth as if by a cosmic rainfall? And what do men and women usually throw into these frightful hollows of life? Some throw wealth, others throw honor and fame, others again throw pleasure and the joy that sears body and soul alike: but the more they throw into them, the hollower they get. For there is a fullness which spells emptiness. We fill our hands with dust, till the very hands that would grasp it turn into dust. We fill our eyes with dust, till there is no vision, only a stupid flicking of tired eyelids. We fill our nostrils with dust, till the breath chokes. We buy dust and we sell dust, and we marry our whole life to dust: what wonder our fullness turns to emptiness? There is but one way to fill the hollows of life: fill it with the emptiness that spells fullness! Fill it with gossamer dreams of beauty, fill it with sheer devotions to truth and goodness at whose insubstantiality the world laughs: ah, throw God into the gaping emptiness and see how full it will become! Give men the assurance that their lives are but part of the infinite life in which they move and have their being; tell them that through God everything they do or design has an infinite worth; tell them that their errors even and their sins, their pains and agonies, are taken up into the being of God, there to find a place of harmony and miraculous accord: tell them that they live in a world where nothing is lost, where no eye weeps and no heart bleeds in vain, and where the feeblest effort at goodness receives infinite support and backing at the hand of the God-who-cares—tell them all this, and you will give them a living faith to satisfy their Great Hunger.

And, lastly, the religion which would answer to this Great Hunger would be one that would raise in the faintest heart the almost impossible hope that the ideal life is possible—that the awful gap between the ideal and the real, between things as they are and as they should be, can be abolished. The highest dreams of mankind can be realized, if men but resolutely turn to the task of realizing them. Contemplation is good, for without it we lack the grace and insight of vision as well as the clarity and consciously directed skill of the understanding. Yet, to the static loftiness of contemplation must be wedded the dynamic drive of action. But, in order that this action be not undertaken half-heartedly, men and women must be assured that the ideal life is possible—and possible not in some remote realm beyond the stars, but here on this brown earth of ours, scene of our activities, cradle of our birth and grave of our last slumber. Utopia is not merely *outopia,* but *eutopia.* It is not merely Erewhon or No-place, it is Somewhere: it is the good and happy place which we shall yet establish here in this valley of our work, in this home of our labors and our loves. Men lack imagination when they think that the present system of civilization—based on barter and trade; on things rather than thoughts; on profits rather than on large concessions; on war rather than on peace and co-operative effort—must continue and endure. They forget the protean resourcefulness of the human soul: how the race can rise to any historic emergency and change its habits and its ways of expression almost indefinitely. The great thing is a large release of life through any mode of expression which renders it possible; and who shall say that the present-day acquisitiveness, having turned the associated life of man into a display of anything but handsomeness, must perdure; that mankind will not find a more generous and more creative form of social existence through which the ideal life may be made the real life here on earth?

Tell men and women that the purpose of religion is to make man at home in this world, until beckoning voices from everywhere invite him familiarly to live the life-in-God, each man under his vine and his fig tree. Tell them that this world is to be built into a home not only for bodies but for souls, for the soul's aspirations, for the soul's deepest longing. Tell them that the last fulfillment of all work and all vision must come through loving service, leading to a progressive perfection of human relations. Progress, automatically conceived, is foolishness. But Progress, as the result of devotion to ideals, of loyalty to man and God, is the highest hope and the highest wisdom of man—the last satisfaction of the Great Hunger.

## IV

This, then, is the meaning of the restlessness of our time: at its heart there is a hunger for God, conceived not as a magician but as a Kindred-Life;

for Truth, not as eternally fixed but as a venture and a discovery; for Human Worth, not found in things adventitious but in Fellowship with God; for a Hope, not grounded in superstition and mythology but in the ineluctable victory of right; and, perhaps most poignantly, for a far-circling Friendliness within whose circumference all children of God might release the measure of their energies.

For the religion which is to answer to the Great Hunger is naught else than a Vast Friendliness in which God and man are companioned together. And because our age is yearning, still dimly, yet in a persistent sort of way, for this kind of religion, therefore let us do it the justice of calling it the Great Age of Faith. The "praisers of bygone times" call this a skeptic age. Not so we. For never has there been such a passion for world friendliness, aye, for cosmic coherence, as in this our day: and never such a resolution to transform the aspect of life into God-likeness. The Great Hunger is upon us: who shall deny it? A mighty wind is blowing through the world: who shall resist it? Hearts are moving in tune with the Infinite: who shall not hope? Great things are coming to pass: the hungry shall be satisfied and the Redeeming Word will be found at last.

# THE CONQUEST OF LIFE

Born in Ohio fifty-five years gone by, Dr. Cavanaugh received both his literary and his theological training in the University of Notre Dame, Indiana, to which much of his life has been devoted as teacher and executive. He was ordained a priest of the Roman Catholic Church in 1894, serving as associate editor of the *Ave Maria Magazine*, as Superior of the Holy Cross Seminary, as professor of English literature in Notre Dame, until 1905, when he became President of the University, a post in which he distinguished himself for fourteen years; after which he taught for a time in Holy Cross College, Washington.

Since 1920 Father Cavanaugh has held the chair of English literature in his Alma Mater, giving a deal of time to the Educational Council and Boy Scout work. Apart from a volume entitled *The Priests of Holy Cross*, issued in 1904, his writing has been chiefly in pamphlets and in religious and literary journals. The following discourse was delivered in the University Church, Notre Dame, at the solemn religious opening of the scholastic year. It recalls the words of Emerson when he said that "the main enterprise of the world for splendor, for extent, is the upbuilding a man," and is all atingle with the stimulating air of youth making ready for the tasks and opportunities of life.

# THE CONQUEST OF LIFE

JOHN CAVANAUGH, C.S.C.

UNIVERSITY OF NOTRE DAME

*I have come that they may have life and may have it more abundantly.* John 10: 10.

"More abundant life!"—the whole purpose of Christ's work is summed up in the phrase. More abundant life for the body, for Christianity has taught men the sacredness of human life, has swept away class distinctions, has struck off the shackles from the slave, has cultivated a fine sense of justice in the general mind; so that whereas in pagan times the master had power over the life and death of servant or child, in Christian times and under Christian teaching there is no man so humble, no cause so weak, no cry so faint, as to be beyond the reach of sympathy or redress.

More abundant life for the soul, for has not Christ established His Church and sent it out on its triumphal course to bind the wounds and heal the sorrows of men, to teach them hidden truth, to open up new realms of thought and new vistas of hope; has he not flooded the minds of men with light and girt them round with divine strength, taught them a new and sublime philosophy—has He not given them the very flowerage of His mind and heart in the seven sacraments which are, after all, the whole of Christianity?

More abundant life for the mind. The Incarnation has made us in a new sense children of God, for it has given us Christ, God's Son, for our Brother. It has made us feel that as God first set man in the heart of paradise and bade him cultivate it and make it fair; as Christ afterwards set paradise in the heart of man and bade him seek it—"The Kingdom of God is within you; seek ye first the Kingdom of God"—so, too, He has given us the kingdom of intellect and bids us go forth like so many explorers with lamps to search its confines. And our heavenly Father looks down on His children as they delve and dig in this kingdom of knowledge, unearthing His mysteries, explaining His plans, unfolding His work adoringly, and He is filled with complacence. Indeed the dignity of culture lies in this, that the more active our minds, the broader and deeper our knowledge, the closer we approach to the Divine Ideal, the clearer becomes the image of God impressed on our souls in creation.

"More abundant life"—the whole of man's aspiration is bound up in the words. To know more, to love more, to feel more, to energize more, to rise to higher vision and purer desire and more courageous action—this is what life means for us from day to day. The savage craves only food and drink and a sharp weapon against the beasts of the forest. As he emerges little by little from the gloom of his cave into the light of civilization, intellect and conscience in him assert themselves more and more over brute force. The development of the race has begun, complex needs arise, aspiration after larger powers and fuller conquest. And what takes place thus slowly in the development of the race takes place more rapidly in each individual of the race even when civilization has most advanced. Every child begins with the elemental craving for food and drink. He speedily develops an interest in the world of sense-perception, and then his life is mostly play; but it is only when he has begun to discipline his mind by study and his will by resisting capricious impulse that he emerges into manhood and claims his inheritance as a child of civilization. Little by little mind in him gains the mastery over matter, and this mastery grows uninterruptedly if he so wills until he becomes the wise man, the Christian sage. Little by little conscience gains the mastery over impulse and this, too, aided by Divine Grace, grows uninterruptedly if he so wills, until he becomes the holy man, the Christian saint. But in every case it is the hunger to love more, the yearning to do more, the courage to resist more—the desire for more abundant life—that stimulates his effort.

You, my dear young men, already know what it is

to aspire after larger life. Some of you in great measure, others in smaller. but all of you in some measure, have come to yearn after knowledge and the power that knowledge gives. In dreams by night and visions by day, angels have come to you, messengers of the Most High King, telling you that you are princes of the blood, bidding you take heart to claim your kingdom. And you have risen up, and girt your loins, and left home and friends—not without many a backward look through misty eyes—to begin the work of conquest. Here to this sanctuary of religion and learning you come to fit yourselves for your kingly office. What can I say to you at the beginning of this school year that will best forward your purpose?

"Three things there are that are hard for me, and the fourth I am utterly unable to understand—the way of an eagle in the air, the way of a ship in the midst of the sea, the way of a serpent on a rock and the way of a man in his youth." So spoke the wisest of the children of men. Youth is the playtime of life. The colt in the pasture, the puppy in the kennel, the kitten on the rug as well as the boy on the campus, are all reminders that youth is largely occupied with play. Far be it from me to find fault with this: youth is the most beautiful season of your lives; once fled it will never come back to you again; and it is a tragedy when youth is clouded with the cares and labors that properly belong to mature manhood. But alas! youth is also the seedtime of life, and what would you say of the farmer who should fritter away the seedtime of the year and still hope for a harvest? Men sometimes talk lightly about the thoughtlessness of youth as if that were a sufficient excuse for neglecting life's serious duties; but if you are ever to be thoughtless, would it not better be in old age when your work is done and when the years are not so heavily freighted with destiny? There is only one time, says Ruskin, when a man can afford to be thoughtless, and that is when he lies on his death-bed. No wise man ever leaves any important thinking to be done there. Recreation and entertainment, then, there must be for youth, but growth too there must be—growth in wisdom, growth in knowledge, growth in strength and courage, growth in faith and hope and love.

And the first lesson you must learn is that the conquest of life is to come through discipline. The most sacred thing in all the world is authority. Authority is the golden ladder whose lowest round rests upon earth, and whose top is bound to the great white Throne of God. The Church of God is built on obedience to authority. The layman obeys his pastor, the pastor obeys his bishop, the bishop obeys the pope, and the pope owes most complete obedience to his Master, Christ. And as man rises in the scale of perfection and of power, the obligations of obedience are multiplied. A superior who is at all fit for the exercise of so holy a function as authority must hold himself ready at all times to serve the lowliest of his subordinates. The Pope is the Vicar of Christ, he is the Successor of Peter, he is the Father of the Faithful, he is the Supreme Pontiff of Christendom, but the title which he recognizes as best fitting his exalted station is this: the Servant of the Servants of God!

And not only in the Church, which is of God's architecture, is obedience to law an absolute necessity, but in all the works of man the principle of obedience to law is paramount. The architect is not free to build according to his whim. Let him ignore the laws of gravity, of resistance or of proportion, and his crooked walls, his unbraced arches, and his top-heavy towers come tumbling down about his head. In nature, too, this law is paramount. "When the river refuses to keep within its banks," says Hillis, "it becomes a curse and a destruction. It is the stream that is restrained by its banks that turns mill-wheels for men. . . . And if disobedience is destruction, obedience is liberty. Obeying the law of steam, man has the steam engine. Obeying the law of fire, he has warmth. Obeying the law of speech, he has eloquence. Obeying the law of sound thinking, he has leadership. Obeying the law of Christ, he has character. . . . As man increases the number of laws he obeys, he increases in richness of nature, in wealth, in strength, in influence. Nature loves paradoxes, and this is her chiefest paradox—that he who stoops to wear the yoke of law becomes the child of liberty, while he who will be free from God's law wears a ball and chain through all his years." St. Paul speaks of "the freedom wherewith Christ has made us free," and what is this freedom but liberty from the yoke of passion through obedience to the law of Christ? Accept the law of God and you become a child of freedom; despise that law and you become the slave of passion. Accept the laws of health and you live a happy, wholesome life; despise them and nature will scourge you with whips of scorpions and plague you with disease. Accept the laws of the commonwealth and you move among your fellows majestic and independent as a king; transgress those laws and you must shun the face of day, and skulk in the darkness like a hunted, hated thing. Wherever you turn, whether to religion or philosophy or history, whether to nature without or conscience within, whether to the health of soul or body, this lesson is written in letters of fire over all the universe: Obey law or die.

The second lesson that you must learn in the conquest of life is that you must discipline the mind by study. One of the saddest facts of life is that the treasures of virtue and learning accumulated by wise and holy men pass out of the world with them; that they cannot be transmitted, as material possessions are, to children and friends. On the other hand, is it not a source of comfort and strength to know that the best things in life, the things that matter, the things that are worth while, may be had by every man on absolutely equal terms? Wisdom, virtue, peace of conscience, knowledge, character—these things cannot be inherited: they must be won by struggle. The temptations you will meet in the practice of obedience and purity are not special to you; they are the common experience of the race. They are as old as the rebellion of Adam, older than the shame of Sodom and Gomorrah. And so the obstacles you will meet in study are the obstacles that have been met and surmounted by all the leaders whose power you so much admire.

> The heights by great men gained and kept
> Were not attained by sudden flight;
> But they while their companions slept
> Were toiling upward in the night.

The greatest advantage you will reap from your college life is in the close association open to you with mellow, cultured minds. Such association will best convince you of the worth of education and will furnish the stimulus needed for self-activity, which is the only true process of education. To lose faith in ideals, in the goodness of knowledge and virtue, is to chill the nerve of effort and to quench the star of aspiration. Let the old and world-worn be pessimists, if they must, but do you cherish the glorious illusions of youth, for only so will you have strength and courage to endure the labor of preparation. "The kingdom of God suffereth violence, and the violent bear it away." The kingdom of knowledge suffereth patience, and the patient bear it away. Learn to work without haste and without worry. Find joy in your work. Labor differs from play only in this, that play is taken up voluntarily and as an end in itself. Look at college boys toiling and groaning in a football scrimmage; then look at weary men heaving bars of iron in the blast-furnace, and tell me: is it not true that the difference between play and toil is a difference wholly within ourselves, a difference in the spirit with which we go to them? Pursue learning, first, because it is a duty which you owe to the father who is willing to stint himself of comforts at home that life may open sweet and large and beautiful on the son whom he loves. Pursue it, too, because in honest study lies your only hope of happiness in college. The slothful student cannot be at peace with himself. Happiness comes from sympathy with one's surroundings. If through idleness you drag along like a hurt or wounded thing far behind your fellows, the classroom, the study hall, the bell of discipline will all bear hard upon you. You will miss the cheery word, the sympathetic glance, the helpful act of professors and disciplinarians. Your school years are indeed a preparation for life, but forget not that they are also a part of life and that they must be lived conscientiously and profitably if you would escape condemnation in the day of final accounting.

A third lesson that you must learn is that the conquest of life is to be wrought by character. God is love, God is mercy, and sins against God may be forgiven. Nature is pitiless, Nature is relentless, Nature is inexorable and if there be a weak spot in your character, Nature will find it out and punish you for it. There have been great temples with towering domes and splendid façades and immortal frescoes that have tumbled down into dust and rubbish because there was a flaw in the foundations. So, too, powerful men of brilliant parts are every day sinking into failure and disgrace and death because of a fundamental flaw in their character. This University is based upon the theory that education is chiefly moral; that character is more than culture. Your Alma Mater will surround you with every strengthening influence that makes for character, but she can work no improvement in you without your coöperation. Christ was the supreme Schoolmaster, but even Christ failed wherever good will and coöperation were wanting among His pupils. Judas, who according to tradition was His playfellow when a boy, who was one of the twelve on whom He lavished all the love of His heart, whom He himself prepared for his first holy Communion on the night of the Last Supper—Judas forgot those years of sweet intimacy and on that very night betrayed his Master for thirty pieces of silver. The lament over the Holy City shows how these failures saddened the heart of our divine Lord. "O Jerusalem! Jerusalem! thou that stonest the prophets, how often would I have gathered thee to my bosom as the hen gathers her young under her wings, and thou wouldst not." And again: "If in Tyre and Sidon had been wrought the things that were wrought in thee, they would long since have done penance in sackcloth and ashes." Christ failed not because He was not the supreme Teacher, not because His doctrine was at fault, but because His hearers by an act of the will deliberately closed their ears against His teaching. He recognized this, and henceforth He ended His lessons with the admonition, "He that hath ears to hear, let him hear." Even so, must your Alma Mater admonish you. Your hearty coöperation for the formation of character is needed if you are to obtain the best results. If only physical constraint operates, if your heart is not in your obedience, in your study and in your religious exercises, you are deliberately shutting yourself out from illumination and strength. Not those whom necessity compels to accept righteousness are blessed, but they who crave for righteousness with an appetite that cannot be satisfied. "Blessed are they that hunger and thirst after justice, for they shall be filled." Unless you are filled with a divine hunger and a divine thirst that will be everywhere and always with you, that will grow with your growth and strengthen with your strength, you have not been educated. Nothing abides but deep conviction. "As a man thinketh in his heart, so is he," says our Lord. That is to say, the measure of a man is the convictions that he cherishes with a love stronger than death.

These, then, are the lessons I would call to your attention on the opening of the new college year. Here in this beautiful temple before the altar whereon is enthroned the Supreme Teacher of mankind, pledge yourself silently during the Holy Mass this morning to live faithful to these ideals. Here among these fields over which holy missionaries, weather-worn and weary, have dragged tired feet, still singing Hallelujahs in their hearts, vow that the sacrifices they have made to create this University shall not have been in vain for you. Here where the sweet smile of Our Lady meets you at the turning of every lane, resolve to cultivate piety and purity in yourselves and to carry the Christian life with you now and forever after wherever you may go. May the benediction of the Most Holy Trinity, Father, Son, and Holy Ghost, rest upon your good resolutions! May the sweet favor of Holy Mary and the strengthening love of the Protector, St. Joseph, be with you and about you always. Amen.

# ANCHORS OF THE DRIVEN SOUL

An Australian of Scotch-Irish ancestry, born in Melbourne in 1885, Dr. McCall entered the Methodist ministry, and soon attracted wide attention by his extraordinary gifts as a preacher. Leaving Australia in 1914 for a year of travel, he was in London when the Great War broke out, and watched the early phases of the struggle in France, Switzerland, and Italy. Returning to his homeland, he took up his work as a minister, but in 1915 left with the Australian troops as preacher and lecturer under the auspices of the Y.M.C.A., serving in Egypt, England, and France—profoundly stirred by the fierce issues, both spiritual and social, involved in the vast tragedy.

After the Armistice he returned to Australia for two years, and in 1921 came to America, as minister of the First Congregational Church of Berkeley, California. His ministry in the University city was a triumph from the beginning, by virtue of its veracity of thought in facing the deep issues of faith and its note of human sympathy, appealing equally to mind and heart; and, best of all, for its suggestion of a "drift of pinions," which, "would we hearken, beats on our clay-shuttered doors." In 1924 he was holiday preacher at the City Temple in London, and made a profound impression, as so many letters from my friends bore glowing witness.

In the autumn of 1924 appeared his book entitled *Cardinals of Faith,* described in its subtitle as a series of "brief studies for a time of groping," which had in it the same qualities of fearless, forthright thinking transfigured by mystical passion, and that undertone of human pity which is the heart of all great preaching, so vividly revealed in the following sermon.

# ANCHORS OF THE DRIVEN SOUL

OSWALD W. S. McCALL, D.D.

FIRST CONGREGATIONAL CHURCH, BERKELEY, CALIFORNIA

*For now we see in a mirror darkly; but then face to face: now I know in part; but then shall I know even as also I have been known. But now abideth faith, hope, love, these three; but the greatest of these is love.*

I Corinthians 13: 12, 13.

After we have said all we may in relief of the problem of suffering, we have done no more than spread a bow of light across the dark face of that perplexing subject. Many and fearful things continue unexplained, things that drive men to madness and that cry out in the sight of heaven for justification, receiving, as far as we can see, none. Even with our best vision we see "in a mirror, darkly," and after our best reasons and discoveries we "know in part" only.

This darkness of imperfect knowledge may be contemplated calmly enough by those to whom trouble is for the time being impersonal. Then, though you may have suffered much in your day, the problem of suffering may nevertheless be speculated upon with abstraction and tranquillity, and your opinions thereupon may be confident and encouraging—if you yourself are temporarily immune from the burn and the pang. As has been said: "Philosophy can gain an easy victory over past and future tribulations, but the present triumph over her."

"Tribulation"—the word was born of the old Roman threshing instrument, the *tribulum,* an instrument still used by certain North Africans to beat the corn from the husks. In coining the word, the Christian thought was that the blows of affliction, raining hard on the soul, would separate the real from the false, the vital from the trivial, until the soul would emerge from its ordeal purged and beautiful. It often happens. Alas, it also happens often that the fierce blows of the soul's tribulum injure the precious wheat itself, until for man the light goes out and a sullen sourness and inhibition creep through the soul that might have sown itself and risen to golden harvests. The results of suffering are not always good.

And it is when the soul quivers beneath blows that are more terrible than it can endure that our imperfect justification of suffering becomes a dangerous thing. Seared and tormented, the soul is apt to turn angrily upon God. "O, my offense is rank, it smells to heaven!" exclaims the murderer of the King of Denmark. But there are tragic moods when the driven soul is ready to cry out that the offense of

God in the earth is ranker and smells up to the heaven of heavens! "I declare—*salva reverentia,*" writes R. E. Welsh, "—I should not like to be God, and hear the cry of pain from the whole conscious creation, and know that I had called such a rueful world into existence. *It would break my heart!*" According to a story I read once, when a certain well intentioned but very ill advised champion of religion wrote conscientiously to a notorious labor leader whose religious opinions were aggressively agnostic, calling upon him to repent of his sins and get right with God ere the Judgment Day should find him unprepared, the agnostic replied caustically: "Brother, though a bigger sinner than you are, I am eagerly looking forward to the Judgment Day. Then whether I shall consent to be right with God will depend upon His answers to some questions I hope to ask."

It may sound daring even unto irreverence, but it is true to certain states of soul, and those states are fraught with peril. Too often souls become like storm-driven ships, groaning terribly in tormenting waves, midnight and no star upon the waters, heights above, deeps beneath, resistless winds driving behind, unknown and disastrous strands awaiting before. "Now we see in a mirror, darkly," and to some the darkness is the most awful pain of all. "Now we know in part," and this imperfect knowledge of the why of things is fearfully dangerous when the soul is being driven and at its wit's end by the following storms of life.

But "now abideth faith, hope, love," and they offer three anchor-holds to the distracted and driven soul.

One is Faith. If any one protests that this is precisely what does not hold in time of tribulation, that it is upon faith the attack of the problem of suffering is most acutely felt, I would reply that I am not so sure. If faith meant placidity I would agree that faith is disturbed: or if faith signified a resignation that can take all that comes without protest, which it does not. Blind resignation is neither faith nor virtue; it is servility. Resignation unto God might be readily made, but frequently enough we are unable to see that it is to God and His will we are asked to yield ourselves.

Let us make this perfectly plain—the dawn of faith is not the end of spiritual strife or perplexity. It might rather be the beginning of it. Dawn is the time of awakening out of sleep, and it presents us with the tasks and problems of the day. It is only as you begin to believe in God that you begin to feel the shock of the things that challenge and deny belief. Who knows but the salmon trout, swimming idly in summer seas, may carry within itself a vague sort of belief in spawning fields far away in the upper reaches of the rivers? But it would not be until its belief sharpens into an attempt to reach those fields that it learns how terrible a thing faith is. Then it discovers the awful argument against faith that that river can advance. If those fields exist, why this resisting rush of water? Why does not the current set toward them instead of away? Why these rapids and barrier cataracts and dangerous shallows? Is there, indeed, anything in all the river to encourage faith? Yet all these difficulties of faith, and the strife, the courage, were never realized until faith became serious and aspiring.

But do not mistake difficulties of faith for absence of faith. Because you feel that every statement of faith ever framed fails to express what you believe; indeed, because you yourself are unable to say what you believe, do not confound statements of faith with faith itself. Remember Tennyson's "faith beyond the forms of faith." *Faith is the soul's knowledge of God as love is our knowledge of one another.* Our love of one another rests not on approval of tricks of speech or look or thought, but on something deeper. The heart deeply interprets and deeply approves the one loved, knows and understands that one better than others do. There may be no argument or even justification possible; many who do not love that one will show you things in speech and manner that seem to belie the hidden worth that your heart has apprehended and loved. Nevertheless, you love; unable to deny the perplexities provoked by some of the loved one's deeds or words, yet you love. Your heart has knowledge of a profounder kind and you say within you: "With all your faults I love you still"—but that is because you somehow know the faults do not fairly represent the truth about your beloved. When we love, our love declares that we have knowledge of our beloved which those do not possess who do not love. Yet ask us how we know, or, indeed, *what* we know, and like lovers since the dawn of time, we shall either stammer foolishly or else plunge into an eloquent enumeration of the virtues and charms of our heart's own—all perfectly true, yet not at all touching the secret of our love nor giving it explanation. Every lover knows that there is a love beyond the forms and verbiage of love, and that love stays though words and evidence sometimes seem to argue that it ought to go. The whole world no doubt scornfully pronounced the prodigal in his rags and penury a wastrel and a sot. Of all the world only the father continued to love him. I suspect the father's knowledge of the boy and his worth was deeper and truer than all the world's: yet not an argument could he pursue and not a shred of evidence could be produce to justify it. Love is our instinctive knowledge of one another.

Likewise, faith is our instinctive knowledge of God. Not built on evidence, often defying evidence, faith, whether it stammers and becomes dumb or breaks into triumphant song, yet clings to Something, Some One Ultimate, whose goodness it affirms.

"Though the fig tree shall not blossom, neither shall fruit be in the vines; the labor of the olive shall fail and the fields shall yield no meat; the flock shall be cut off from the fold, and there shall be no herd in the stalls"—all that is the evidence of divine goodness—the distressing evidence!—open to the prophet Habakkuk—"Yet I will rejoice in the Lord, I will joy in the God of my salvation"—that is the ascent of the soul to the faith that is behind and beyond evidence, the faith that instinctively feels that God is good in His own right and because He is God, not because of evidence; that the things which bewilder explanation are but fragments, whereas the soul has a deeper knowledge of its Maker, on the strength of which it will exonerate Him though all evidence seem to condemn. Problems of faith have been from the beginning, yet has faith flourished, the religion of the earth bearing testimony to the soul's "assurance of things not seen."

It is by no means a trivial thing for the soul to be able to state what it thinks about God; but in distraught and harassed hours every word of faith may seem mocked or foolish. In such hours let your soul dispute with heaven if it will, daringly, even angrily, yet let it never dispute irreverently. Like Job, bring forth your complaint and debate with God. Perchance you will conclude where he did, dumb, not because of arguments answered but because of the soul's mystic affirmation of the integrity of God.

Realize *that* faith and you will have achieved an anchor for the storm.

There also "abideth Hope." Faith has been described as the upward and hope as the forward look of the soul. Certainly hope is the soul's optimism. But the soul ready to be engulfed in the black maw of despair is more likely to be incensed than cheered by any easy advice to be hopeful. Is it not often the hopelessness of the outlook that makes the suffering cruelest, and shall we be invited to force a hopefulness that all proclaims to be groundless? This would be to trifle with the soul, offering it comfort by pretending facts to be other than they are.

The hope which God invites us to is not so shallow. Aristotle defined hope as "a waking dream." If the first impulse is to dismiss all dreams as made of less toughness than air, a moment's reflection will give them more significance than that, for *dreams are made of experience.* However fantastic may be the tapestry, every thread has been drawn from the looms of life. The content of your dream would have been different had you been brought up in a different land or in a different age—yes, had your experience of heart and mind been different. And is hope "a waking dream"? Its significance, then, lies in all that experience of life and things which is behind the hope. If life had not given cause for optimism we should not hope. If our experience had not been full of doors opening in unexpected places, of "hair-breadth 'scapes" from deadly impasse, of good emerging incredibly from ill, and of songs arising after sighing, we should never hope. The dreams of hope are backed by the life story of the race—a story joyously laden with deliverances, and with the heart's prizes won at last.

This is the stuff that hope's dreams are made of. Because, in the past, life has shown itself to be a thing not heaven-forsaken, it becomes reasonable to expect it not to be forsaken in the future. Hope does not drug the soul until it comforts itself with futile dreams that can never come true. Rather it lights a torch at the fires of truth as they burn in the sub-conscious treasures of a man, and with that lighted torch it cheers the present and the future. The shrubs of our desire are stricken stark by the wintry frosts of affliction, but a breath blows out from our heaven-blessed past and touches the leafless, bloomless branches until they burst in beauty, and we call it hope. There is vital connection between our hope of the future and our experience of the past. It is not a mere comfortable folly, nor is it a baseless assuaging of pain, when the psalmist again and again rises above his complaints to cry: "Why art thou cast down, O my soul? and why art thou disquieted within me? Hope thou in God, for I shall yet praise Him." "And this hope we have as an anchor of the soul."

But a third is Love—not here the affection of

father or lover or child, but the Christian law of kindness and fellowship. The immense, almost rugged, nature of this chief Christian ethic, love, may bear upon the mind better if we recall Professor Rauschenbusch's definition of it: "No flickering or wayward emotion, but *the energy of a steadfast will bent on creating fellowship.*" For instance, Christ's requirement that we should "love our enemies" becomes impossible of achievement if Love is an emotion; for I am simply unable to feel affectionate toward a man who has done me some bitter wrong. But if, instead, love is under the control of the will, and is a moral attitude, determined, somehow, to create fellowship, I can, even in defiance of my natural impulse to antagonism, bend myself to the winning of the man who has wronged me. Similarly, nations can override hereditary dislikes and, with a sustained energy of will, study and do the things that make for fellowship. This, then, is the very practical and enormously redeeming ethic upon which Christ placed his supreme emphasis.

Paul does well to name this as "the greatest of these," for though Faith should wither and Hope depart, we should still be unabsolved from the obligations of Love. Here the soul is held. Neither doubt nor despair can set one free from the command of love. Rid the mind of sentimentality here, even of emotionalism, and leave love as character's cardinal ethic; see love as the opposite of selfishness; see it as a cool and deliberate will to fellowship, an endeavor toward right relationships. Then may we realize that here is both the most virile and the most promiseful challenge ever presented to the soul. Faith or hope apart, the obligation to live decently and considerately with our fellow men never relaxes. Though your heart is being tormented, it is still your business to escape self-pity and to remember there are other hearts than yours in the world. Though you fall on some bleak tract clean forspent, yet does that not give you permission to become a misanthrope. Doubt your God if you must, despair of the future if you must, but, in peril of your soul, see that no shadow fall between you and your fellow men! Here, at least, the light is clear.

I tell you that if you will accept this obligation to live with open heart toward your fellows; if you will parry the inducement to renounce this great ethic in favor of something less, something confined and self-seeking in spirit, you will have found an anchor that will hold though the hawsers of faith and hope part under strain. On this one cable you will ride out the storm.

Therefore, in the midst of life's hard problems we lift up our head to hear sounding in our ears as the loudest note, not the command to Believe, nor the invitation to Hope, but the stern voice of Duty—"Thou shalt love!" Probably it is only as we hear this voice and obey that either faith or hope can live.

Find me a great sufferer with his faith and his hope in ruins, but a sufferer who also has been a great lover of his kind, forgetting not to be gracious, disowning not his ministry, and I think I shall be able to point you at last to his faith climbing high like a tower of jasper, its base broad-set in character, its forehead heaven-kissed—and about it, hope, blooming like the Garden of the Lord.

"Stern Daughter of the Voice of God," is Wordsworth's description of duty. I leave you looking out upon a granite prospect. Are you able for this? Whether you are or not, cast off your shoes, for this ground is holy. Here the saints of the earth have walked—humble men, often, but brave, who have seen that of "faith, hope, love, the greatest of these is love"—the greatest, the sublimest, the least escapable and the final obligation of the soul.

As a great teacher reminds us, the question that faces us all over the gateway of life is—"Wilt thou be a hero or a coward?" Dare to make this noble ethic yours and out of your enriched life all faith and hope may grow. Be sure such sublimities cannot arise from unworthy character. Get right with man—and it may not be long ere you will find yourself right with God.

# GIANTS AND GRASSHOPPERS

Bishop McConnell has a place all his own in the American church, both as a thinker and as a Christian statesman. He unites in rare degree spiritual insight, practical capacity, and disinterested courage, which Emerson held to be the qualities of real greatness. By the votes of more than twenty thousand preachers he was recently selected as one of the twenty-five most influential preachers in America: but we did not need a vote to tell us that.

Born in Ohio in 1871, an alumnus of Ohio Wesleyan University and of Boston University, he entered the Methodist ministry in 1894. After several pastorates in New England, he came to the New York Avenue Church, Brooklyn, in 1903. Six years later he was elected to the presidency of De Pauw University, from which position he was called to the high office of Bishop in 1912. He is one of the great leaders of Christian thought and enterprise in America, his influence and power extending far beyond the bounds of his own communion.

Of a long list of books by Bishop McConnell, none has been more helpful than his essay on *Religious Certainty,* unless it be his lectures on *Living Together.* In *The Preacher and the People* and *Public Opinion and Theology* he has to do with the problems of the pulpit; while in *The Divine Immanence* and *Is God Limited?*—his latest book—he deals with the form which the thought of God takes in the mind of our time. In the following sermon he talks to us familiarly, as is his manner, of a certain tendency in human nature to disguise cowardice in a plausible conservatism—a message much needed betimes.

# GIANTS AND GRASSHOPPERS

FRANCIS J. McCONNELL

BISHOP OF THE METHODIST CHURCH, PITTSBURGH

*And there we saw the giants, the sons of Anak, which come of the giants; and we were in our own sight as grasshoppers, and so we were in their sight.* Numbers 13: 33.

The text is taken from the story of the advance of the Hebrews to the Promised Land. Moses had sent twelve men ahead to spy out Canaan and they had come back with their report. Upon one thing the entire band of scouts at first agreed. They declared the land to be flowing with milk and honey. Then a man named Caleb came plumply out with the recommendation to move *at once* into the land. That put matters in a different light. The students of this passage about the spies have always been puzzled to see how the same persons who declared the land to be flowing with milk and honey in one verse could have declared the land to be an evil land in almost the next verse. They have thought that perhaps two differing traditions have been preserved here and woven into one account. We may well believe this if good and sufficient reasons are advanced, but it does not seem to us that this change of description of Canaan is conclusive. The suggestion of Caleb comes in between the contradictory opinions. It was the thought of moving straight to the attack which changed the opinion of the ten scouts.

Human nature was the same back in those days as it is today. A change in the inner attitude made a change in the outward appearance. As long as the scouts were not confronted with the immediate possibility of assailing the land of Canaan they saw the milk and honey. The very suggestion, however, to march to forthright attack so withered their inner spirit that in their thought the land withered also. An inner drought made them imagine an outer drought. The ten belonged to that large class of human beings to whom the Promised Land looks pleasant until you urge them to capture it *now*. Then difficulties develop. There is no doubt in our day that, if the people would, we could introduce large elements of the millennium tomorrow morning, but ten out of twelve who sing about the delights of the kingdom of God on earth and who pray devoutly for the coming of the kingdom might be horror-struck at the idea of immediately moving into the Promised Land. Too speedy advance might have a bad effect on business, or on something else. The fields might eat up the inhabitants thereof. No—there is nothing incredible in the idea that those who praised the land in verse 27 of Numbers 13 cursed it in verse 32. Caleb's suggestion is in verse 30.

The ten scouts give the reason for their own distress in their view of themselves. "We were in our own sight as grasshoppers." Since they took themselves as grasshoppers, it is only natural that the inhabitants of the land should have taken them as grasshoppers. If a man takes himself as a grasshopper, he need not be surprised if the onlookers speedily acquiesce in his view. Quite likely these ten scouts acted like grasshoppers, bending over to conceal themselves and leaping along in dire terror of the giants—no doubt to the huge amusement of the giants themselves. The situation would seem almost humorous if it were not so often repeated. The grasshopper view of human life is not yet banished from human thought. When we begin to urge men to enter the Promised Land which God holds out before us we are often met with the cry: "Alas, we are but grasshoppers! How can frail creations like ourselves attain unto such victory? How can we conquer the immense physical forces around us? How can we so modify economic conditions as to establish the kingdom of God here on earth? The ideal is glorious, but 'we are as grasshoppers in our sight.' And we are as grasshoppers in the sight of the social and industrial giants who are now monopolizing the milk and honey!" And, as of old, the grasshopper view of human life is followed by the grasshopper conduct.

Caleb did not care much for the grasshopper doctrine. He was not appalled by the mere size of the inhabitants of Canaan. He had a different creed concerning himself. He knew that the spiritual element is what counts in a real struggle for a Promised Land, and he was willing to match the spirit of Israel against the mere size of the inhabitants of Canaan. He knew the power of the consciousness of the nearness of the Lord as a fighting factor on the field of battle. Caleb had the right of it. The victories which Israel won were all won by the emphasis on the spiritual factor. Jericho fell, simply because of the irresistible conviction of Israel that it must fall. When the Israelites forgot God they dropped quickly back to the grasshopper stage. All their power was in their spiritual audacity. The formal reasons were indeed in favor of staying behind. The majority had statistics and measurements on their side. They knew how tall the inhabitants were and how many there were of them. Caleb and Joshua simply said that the people should go forward at once, for they were well able to possess the land,—but this was opinion, and not statistics. The statistics were in favor of staying at a distance. That is one trouble with statistics. Too often there is no suggestion of "go" in them. Caleb said that the people ought to go ahead. About all the important movements in the world's life have come as some leader has encouraged the people to go ahead in face of all the facts which can be brought against advance. It is easy to find ten reasons against advance for one in favor of advance.

The people wailed all night. The voice of the people, even of the peculiar people chosen to do the work of the Lord, could hardly have been called the voice of God on this particular occasion. After a period of incoherent weeping somebody raised the question as to what should be done under the circumstances! When they came face to face with this question there were just three things that could be done; first they could stay where they were, but that did not seem promising; second, they could listen to Caleb and advance to the Promised Land, but that suggestion aroused them to madness; third, they could go back to Egypt. When we think about these alternatives we are struck again with the fact which we have so often observed, namely, that, after all, the plan of the Lord is the only plan which will work, in spite of all the formal reasons that can be marshaled against it. As soon as the thought of going back to Egypt arose there arose also the question as to how to get back. These people had been moving through the desert without taking any thought of the paths. There would have hardly been a safe guide among them apart from some one whom Moses might select. The people had been trudging along without paying much attention to where they were. All they thought of was food—and changes of food. They knew that they could not get back without a leader. Then they set themselves for the selection of a captain. But who should be the captain? Manna does not seem to have been particularly palatable to the people, but could they be sure that the new captain could get even that? It came in the end about to this—that the only man they could rely upon was Moses, and the only safe plan was to go ahead. When Joshua and Caleb again urged this plan, however, the people were willing to stone them. No better word could have been spoken than the words of those who were willing to go ahead. It is a principle of any warfare that the moral element is to the physical element as about three to one; and Caleb, though he did not have as many reasons as the others, had the weighty reason after all. "The Lord is with us, and not with them." "Their defense is departed from them." "The battle is over before it has begun." "Let us go up at once." All these words are the words of a real leader. Caleb sees that the favor of the Lord and the consciousness of his presence mean more than mere muscle. Assuming that there were giants in the land, the giants were not so tall as to be able to overcome the moral superiority of the believers in the Lord. Very few physical giants amount to anything. And Caleb would start at once. Every day in the wilderness meant greater demoralization of the force. It was all good sense and deep piety—which, by the way, always belong together.

Caleb was overwhelmingly voted down, but he received the promise of an entrance into the land of Canaan nevertheless. It is a remarkable illustration of the way in which a vote which is not counted at the time may be counted afterwards. Caleb's insistent appeal for immediate advance came to nothing at the time except great uproar among the people. Those who kept their heads at all may have thought Caleb a very foolish fellow in not moving to make the report of the ten unanimous. He ought to work in quieter ways, they may have said. If he accedes now, we shall be spared this uproar. Caleb is "setting the cause back," for the more he protests as to the good of the land the more the ten protest as to its barrenness. Caleb means well, but he is not as wise as he might be. Caleb as a matter of actual fact did accomplish nothing at the time. His vote was thrown out, as was that of the faithful Joshua who sided with him. A vote for advance to the work of the Lord, however, is not thrown away. There is another set of tellers than those who actually appear on earth. The Lord counts votes and he counts them not quantitatively but qualitatively. In the eyes of the Lord the vote of Caleb and Joshua was the only worthy result of the expedition of the spies. He promised reward to these men who had brought nothing to pass except to make a commotion. The ten had their way. The wise heads who deplored the lack of discretion in Caleb and Joshua applauded the ten. The people said fine things about desiring to protect their wives and little ones and not straining the established order, and finally bade one another stone Caleb and Joshua "with stones." Probably they thought themselves very lenient that they eventually spared the lives of such reckless radicals. But the day of Joshua and Caleb came later, and when that day came the ten and the people who had shouted their approval of their disparaging report had died like grasshoppers in the wilderness which they had voted not to leave.

This seems like a hard fate—this death of the doubters in the wilderness, but the simple fact was that the people who had lived long in Egypt were not fit for the Promised Land. They were too old —old not so much in years as in their proneness to look backward. As the days and weeks and months and years had gone by, the harsh features of the service in Egypt had become softened in their recollections. They forgot the long hours, the dark mornings when they had to get up before daybreak and hunt straw for the bricks, the lash of the taskmaster, and the exactions of Pharaoh. All they could see was that they were having a hard time of it in the wilderness, and Egypt looked pleasant by contrast. There was no need of thinking of advancing into Canaan with such an incurably backward-looking people. So the whole generation had to die off.

History is always repeating itself. Some Canaans

never can be entered until the generation that first hears of Canaan passes off the stage, and a new generation comes which knows not Egypt. The children of the Israelites, born in the wilderness, did not suffer from the backward glance. All they knew was the wilderness and the prospects of Canaan. The leeks and the onions and the garlic about which they heard their parents talk meant nothing to them. Accustomed to hard fare in the wilderness, they would not have known an onion if they had seen it. Moreover, the very hardness of the training fitted them for conquest. The generation that came out of Egypt served the Lord by coming out of Egypt. Possibly that was enough for them. Physically they wrought a great service in getting out of Egypt. Spiritually they never really got out; their minds kept always turning back. The decree that they must perish was not arbitrary. They never could have got into the Land of Promise, and if they had they could not have stayed. In the light of the aftertimes we see that they served by getting out of Egypt. The younger generation had to do the getting into Canaan.

Those who came out of Egypt were bound to see the dark side of Canaan. They said that the land was a bad land and that it ate up the inhabitants thereof. Then these reporters of course went on to say that the inhabitants of Canaan were giants. Just how the land could at one and the same time eat up the inhabitants and cause those inhabitants to grow to the stature of giants does not appear. A little inconsistency like that does not bother a people looking back to Egypt. We have no historical records that the peoples in Canaan at the time of the coming of Israel were of such enormous stature as to warrant calling them giants. The spies in their panic added a foot or two to the height of the Canaanites. They didn't see double but they did see ordinary height exaggerated into giantlike stature. All this was honest enough. Nobody was telling any lies. What a man sees depends not only on his eyes but also on what is back of his eyes. Back of the Egypt-born eyes was an old, despairing mental habit that never would have seen anything good in Canaan.

"We were in our own sight as grasshoppers, and so we were in their sight," said the majority report of the spies. Very likely! If a man takes himself as a grasshopper he need not complain if other people take him as a grasshopper. If a man takes himself as a grasshopper he is likely to act like a grasshopper. That is the way these hankerers after Egypt probably acted, squatting down in terror on the ground and hopping like insects from the shelter of one bush to another. When a man is squatting close to the ground, any man standing up on his two feet looks to the squatter like a giant. What a spectacle it is—the advance agents of the chosen people of God, the descendants of Abraham, the forefathers of the

Christ, the called to world destiny,—sneaking around on their hands and knees in the grass and calling the Canaanites giants!

It was all very ridiculous but not one whit more ridiculous than the present day pessimism which admits that Christian principles applied to society, to government, to industry would lead to a Land of milk and honey, but which wails in distress at the idea of doing anything now. Let us trust to the slow processes of education; let us see if we cannot breed giants of our own in the wilderness; let us see if we cannot starve one Canaanite giant at a time into surrender. At some periods in social advance such advice is wise—but at other periods the call should be for immediate advance. Some massive improvements in the political, social, industrial realms could be seized at once if a given generation would listen to Caleb and Joshua. Since that generation will not listen we give ourselves to the training of a new generation,—and meantime the old generation dies off.

We can lift the lesson out of the Old Testament altogether and bring it down to a present-day setting. The Christ whom we serve is a lord of harvests as well as of seed sowings. When any harvests of truth ripen for individual and social applications his word is that his followers should *immediately* put in the sickle. Some advances should be sounded *now*. To postpone, or to hesitate, is to resist an essentially Christian impulse.

# THE THINGS THAT ARE EXCELLENT

An arresting article in the *Century Magazine,* February, 1922, entitled "A Famine of Prophets," first made Mr. Krumbine widely known outside of his own communion. It was a plea, at once pointed and persuasive, in behalf of the adventurous spirit of youth, as over against gray-haired men and gray-haired ideas, in the leadership of the church: a thesis fortified by the facts of history, as well as by the plight of the church in the wake of the World War. After reading such an article, one watched for anything else from the same pen.

Two years later followed a volume of sermons, entitled *The Way to the Best,* such a book as one finds only once in a great while and reads more than once. The note was unmistakable, and one knew not which to admire most, its mastery of the art of sermon structure or its wealth of wise and forward-looking truth nobly uttered; its rich allusiveness, its poise of style, or its maturity of insight and judgment. Hardly any first book of recent years has given more promise of what is now so much needed—a leadership of wisdom and vision.

A Pennsylvanian, born thirty-four years ago, Mr. Krumbine was educated in Albright and Gettysburg colleges, and in the Lutheran Theological Seminary at Gettysburg, with later studies in the University of Wisconsin; and since 1918 he has been pastor of the First Lutheran Church of Dayton, Ohio. The sermon here to be read was delivered at the University of Chicago in June, 1925.

# THE THINGS THAT ARE EXCELLENT

MILES H. KRUMBINE

FIRST LUTHERAN CHURCH, DAYTON, OHIO

*That ye may approve the things that are excellent.*
Philippians 1: 10.

This whole letter to the Philippians gains added force when we remember the circumstances under which it was written. Paul is a prisoner in Rome. The issue is exceedingly doubtful. The emperor is none other than Nero. He may be expected to have little sympathy with such a man as Paul. Moreover, Paul is soon to go on trial for his life and work before this very Nero. Whatever word he would write at such a time would have the dew of death upon it. He wrote the letter to the Philippians at that time.

The little church at Philippi is Paul's first congregation in Europe. His letter to them is an intimate and artless piece of writing. It is a chatty note, glowing with the warmth of personal affection. "Rejoice," is its prevailing note. Paul writes out of the fullness of his heart to these folks whom he loves and who love him. He is proud of this little group. They maintain the simplicity and purity of their lives in the midst of an environment that is corrupting.

Paul's joy is tempered with a real concern; his hopefulness weighted down with a sense of the difficulty ahead. In the very first paragraph he gives away the secret yearning of his heart for them, "that ye may approve the things that are excellent." The future is certain if his dear Philippians can keep alive the faculty of discrimination and discernment; if they can continue to appreciate and undertake the excellent.

Consider, for a moment, what that meant in the society of that day. Anybody who has read a little mythology knows that the most obvious facts of life suggested all manner of low and degrading thoughts to the pagan. His cultural background and environment furnished him with gods and goddesses a plenty, symbolizing all too frequently that which is mean and base. If a citizen of that world went out under the starry sky at night he found erotic legends scrawled across it.

> We know [writes Chesterton] what sort of sentimental associations are called up to us by the phrase "a garden"; and how we think mostly of the memory of melancholy and innocent romances, or quite as often of some gracious maiden lady or kindly old person pottering under a yew hedge, perhaps in sight of a village spire. Then let any one who knows a little Latin poetry recall suddenly what would once have stood in place of the sundial or the fountain, obscene and monstrous in the sun; and of what sort was the god of their gardens.

The environment which the early Christian community inherited in a city such as Philippi "flattered the passions in the name of heaven." Their heaven and their earth was defiled and polluted. The things that are excellent, as Paul appraised excellence, were not easily distinguished and less easily approved.

The long swing of the historic process has again made this letter a contemporary document. The excellent way of life is again a blur. Desirable as is the goal of the Christian life, there is a great debate about the way thereto. Possessed of meat and drink, shelter and entertainment, we, in this rich, glorious, avaricious America, are finding it alarmingly easy to become reconciled to almost anything. We are seeing high personal integrity sent into retirement in our group life. The vulgar is taken to be necessary while what is customary is considered right and proper. Our critical powers and our moral discernment are held in abeyance while the "Victorian dikes" are breaking. Ailing youth has become infected from its environment of sickened age. A passion to be average has stifled the resolve to be excellent. To do good has displaced the will to be good. "Few men and women of first-class intellectual ability and first-rate spiritual magnitude," wrote the editor of the *Saturday Review,* at the opening of 1925, "feel the compulsion to be great. The fashionable illusion now is of importance, a very different thing, with very different effects, and a habit of inflating the second-rate." Verily, Paul is writing to us "that ye may approve the things that are excellent."

What then, we may well ask, are these excellent things that we are asked to approve? To what is Paul urging us to commit our lives? The passion to be excellent must of necessity nourish itself, and so fulfill itself, on the things that are excellent. For our answer we turn to the extended moral experience of Paul himself as it is laid out for us in his writings.

## I

Humility is one of these things that are excellent. One hesitates to speak of humility in the modern world where the advertising value of men and things exceeds their real value. And yet what word is more needed than the word "Be humble"?

St. Paul, the magnitude of whose labors covered the civilized world (and the end is not yet), described himself quite honestly as "less than the least of the apostles." With a world to change and a social order to renew, he followed the Master's way in meekness and lowliness of heart. Humble tasks, humble folk, a humble habit of life became the foundation of a world-winning movement. The winsomeness of a Christian soul which gave life and victory to a revolutionary movement was refreshed from the spring of genuine humility that flowed increasingly in his heart.

But what is humility? A willful depreciation of one's powers? Hardly. Said Dürer to his critic, "In all the world it cannot be done better." And Dürer was humble. Doubt of one's powers? There is no triumph in that. "It is absurd in any review," wrote Shelley, "to criticize *Adonais,* still more to pretend that the verses are bad. I know what to think of *Adonais,* but what to think of those who confound it with the many bad poems of the day, I know not." And Shelley "loved everything better than himself." Humility is the deliberate recognition of God as the source of our strength, skill, and power. "I can of myself do nothing," cried Jesus. "I can do all things through Him who strengtheneth me," wrote the humble Paul. Humility is the frank and full acknowledgment of unnecessary imperfection in our work even after a period of unremitting toil. What exquisite skill went into the making of Katherine Mansfield's stories, what labor she gave to them! Just before her death she wrote, "There is not one of them that I dare show to God." Humility is an excellent thing.

Two vices are bringing down the modern world as the envenomed sting of the snake brings down the eagle. The one is the growing belief that man's chief good is bound up with the secular interests of his life. There is an insistent passion to improve the world we are living in which animates the finer spirits, but that improvement usually stops with the secular, the physical status of man. Religion has been found to be a ready handmaid to the secular interests of life, as Professor Jacks foresaw. Today practical religion, so called, is housing more people, feeding more people, clothing more people than ever heretofore. It is stamping out poverty, crime, and disease. But it leaves the moral issues, whence spring wars, famines, and pestilences, severely alone. The other vice springs directly from this practical achievement. The very effectiveness of human effort to relieve the sufferings and forward the secular aspirations of man has created a suspicion that human effort is all that is needed. Divine aid as a necessary force for human improvement, which is the nerve of religion, is today, if not found entirely unnecessary, certainly not one of man's most conscious needs. The triumphant skill of the scientist, the ready wit of the philanthropist, the practical good sense of the parish priest, combined with the world-conquering career of the industrialist, have united to silence the cry to God for help. Humility is a difficult virtue, indeed, for men seem so very able.

Will mankind be safe, will the very secular interests so dear to us be secure before such strength, untouched by a sense of humbleness before God? Is not the very difference between Paul and Nero one of humility before God? The pagan Pythagoras, we are told, offered a sacrifice to the gods in joy at a mathematical discovery. Then how much more ought the modern man of skill and genius to turn to his God in humble adoration and thanks!

## II

Courage is another of the things that are excellent. Paul had it in abundance. When the vision broke upon him his immediate response was, "Lord, what wilt Thou have me to do?" To see his duty was with Paul to do it. His courage always closed the gap between thinking and doing. "But I will tarry at Ephesus until Pentecost," he writes the Corinthians, "for a great door and effectual is opened unto me *and there are many adversaries*." Hesitation, delay, retreat, flight—these words are not found in the vocabulary of Paul.

There are three kinds of courage. First, we have the Greek virtue of courage. It is confined almost entirely to valor in battle, Professor Mackenzie assures us, and has but little correspondence to anything that is supremely important in modern life. Again, we have the courage of endurance, commonly called fortitude. "It bears pain rather than goes to risk it; it bows to the inevitable rather than carve out a destiny for itself." It is passive endurance, helpless bravery before evils that seem overwhelming. When the Christian cause was a minority movement the virtue of fortitude under persecution was of supreme importance. The third phase of courage fits our modern situation far better: Courage is "a gallant spirit throwing itself into a worthy cause"; it is an aggressive attempt by men and women of capacity to improve, reform, redeem life. Courage in a day like ours means once more leaving house and brethren and lands for Christ's sake and the Gospel's. Courage in a social order "where wealth accumulates and men decay" means again the rash renunciation of a Francis of Assisi, the burning eloquence of a Savonarola, and the on-going toil of a Wesley. Ideals need again, as in Philippi of old, to be preached and lived so vividly that they can become recreative in the life of the day.

That will require courage. Mankind today is not blessed with an excess of that virtue. Christianity has fallen into the hands of interpreters who have toned down for us its hard demands. For the trumpet call to take up our cross and follow we have been offered the soothing chants of a beautiful ritual. For the sublime offer of Jesus, "What things soever ye desire, when ye pray, believe that ye receive them and ye shall have them," we are offered entertaining treatises on the psychology of prayer. Meanwhile the "simplicity of the prayers of Jesus remains undisturbed by any shadow of doctrinal reflection." For the meaningful verities of the Sermon on the Mount we are shown the discouraging baseness of human conduct. We are supposed to assume that therefore Jesus could not have meant it for a world such as ours. For the uneasiness of an aroused conscience we are still offered the mental soporific of a traditional theology. All of which serves to dull the edge of our courage, to set back the day of resolution, to unman us for the good, hard thinking, the brave decisive living that must be done before modern life can be soundly Christian.

"Christianity is constantly verifying itself," writes Cairns, "in the experience of those who believe it," those who take it seriously. It is that verification that is convincing, a verification of life more than a demonstration of the intellect. We face our own specific call to live the daring life, even as the martyr ages faced theirs and the ages of the doctrinal controversies theirs.

> Grant us the will to fashion as we feel,
> Grant us the strength to labor as we know,
> Grant us the purpose, ribb'd and edg'd with steel,
> To strike the blow.
>
> Knowledge we ask not,—knowledge Thou hast lent,
> But, Lord, the will—there lies our bitter need,
> Give us to build above the deep intent
> The deed, the deed.

## III

The most obvious, as it was the most moving, motive that played upon the life of Paul was his unfailing loyalty to Jesus. "I live, yet not I, Christ liveth in me"; "that with all boldness . . . Christ shall be magnified in my body either by life or by death. For to me to live is Christ and to die is gain." It is easy to set aside these passages as having no practical value for our lives on the ground of an irrational mysticism. Their practical moral force, when viewed from the standpoint of a compelling loyalty to Christ, is unmistakable. "There can be no doubt," says Deissmann in his very learned study of Paul, "that St. Paul became influential in the world precisely by the reason of his mysticism about Christ. The spiritual Christ was able to do what a dogmatic Messiah never could have done." Certainly his mysticism was touched with a moral sobriety and enthusiastic sincerity that fashioned it into a force for righteousness in his time. And if today some of the phrases of Paul seem strangely overdrawn, may it be because we have permitted our fellowship with Christ to become petrified into a dogma about Christ? There was still vivid in the life of Paul that primitive sense of intimacy with Christ which assured the Christian movement success from its very start. That we can find fault with the way Paul expressed it after centuries of rationalizing and dogmatic controversy doesn't at all reduce the fact, either in importance or in pertinence. There we see the ancient apostle so dominated by his sense of loyalty to Christ and the things for which he stood that he becomes irresistible in the most unfriendly, yea, and in the dullest environment.

Loyalty is one of the things that are excellent, not chiefly for what it makes us able to do, but for what it does for us. To how many humble souls, yea, and exalted souls, too, is Christianity a very simple matter of loyalty to Jesus up to the level of their powers! They know little and care less about the sinuous mental meanderings of the learned mind; they take discouragingly little interest in the established institutions of religion; they content themselves with a more or less sincere attempt to square their conscience with "the good man," to be as decently wholesome as the pressure of life and the moral tone of the environment permits. The steadying influence that this ideal of loyalty has is incommensurable.

Consider the lifting power of loyalty. Loyalty lifted Paul from the confining pit of bigotry and sent him abroad a friend to mankind. Loyalty took the untamed life of Francis of Assisi and by passing it through the crucible of utter renunciation made it lovely as a poem, an embarrassing challenge to modern life, in the name of Christ. We praise Lincoln; we praise and we wonder. Upon what meat did this, our Lincoln, feed that he grew so great? It remained for Tolstoi to give us the clue, who, when the great Emancipator died, wrote, "Lincoln was a Christ in miniature." The history of literature records one of the most amazing examples of the lifting power of a great loyalty known to man. Young James Boswell, as we now see him in Professor Tinker's book, came down to London from his native Scotland "an idler, a lecher, a drunkard, and a snob." At twenty-three he met Dr. Samuel Johnson. A year later he was writing to him at Wittenberg, "from the tomb of Melanchthon": "My paper rests upon the gravestone of that great and good man. At this tomb then, my ever dear, respected friend, I vow thee an eternal attachment." The rest of Boswell's existence was the history of that vow's accomplishment. The result is the greatest biography in English and an undying fame for this "idler, lecher, drunkard, and snob."

To cherish an inner loyalty to the Christ is to put oneself in the way of having one's whole life recreated. "Ye must be born again," urged Jesus, not in a physical way, but spiritually, or, as we might say, psychologically. Such spiritual rebirth was a new idea in Jesus' day. Nicodemus was properly perplexed by it. The Christian Church has more or less professed belief in it. For the most part, however, we have been content to make very little of it. Today the new psychology is urging this very principle of rebirth upon us as a necessary step to spiritual health and well-being. One of its commonest teachings is the transference of old emotions to a new object, thereby creating new sentiments, new habits, a new way of living. The healing power of psychology inheres largely in this very process. But is it not only another way of proclaiming the power of loyalty? Are we not being reminded, in the name of this new and precocious science, of the life-giving value, the moral excellence of loyalty to Christ? For who that ever lived is more worthy to be the center of our emotional life? How, indeed, can those who live in ancient Philippi, or in modern Main Street, save themselves from polluting contact with a culture in decay, or the peril of drabness, unless they recenter their lives in loyalty to Jesus, who is to us as the vine is to the branches, our source of moral health and the vitality of our spiritual culture.

## IV

Finally, one may fairly add "enthusiasm for the best" to this catalogue of the things that are excellent. "That ye may become blameless—children of God without blemish in the midst of a crooked and perverse generation among whom ye are seen as lights in the world." This is the prayer of Paul for his Philippians. "For many walk, of whom I told you often, and now tell you even weeping, that they are enemies of the Cross of Christ; whose end is perdition, whose God is their belly, and whose glory is in their shame, who mind earthly things." With an eye single to the excellence of his friends, Paul is keenly mindful of the deadly lure of tangible pleasures, the seductive pull of the popular manner of life. He craved for his own a consuming enthusiasm for the best.

There is perhaps little in the writings of Paul of what we now call the social gospel. Paul *was* the social gospel. Wherever he went superstitions were laid, customs changed, evil interests that fed on society like a cancer were uprooted. At Ephesus something like a social revolution ensued upon his preaching. At Thessalonica he was charged in court with turning the world upside down. At Corinth he was thrust before the proconsul for showing men a better way. Always he found himself in conflict with prevailing social complacency for the sake of the best. Paul was the social gospel because his heart was socialized. There was in him that faculty of social imagination which led him straight to the task of social redemption most needed to be done.

We are all moved by a certain enthusiasm for the best, or what Jesus called the Kingdom of God. We are at least willing to see the best prevail, to have the right win. We are not always willing to help the right win, to make the best prevail. We are all eager to see our world changed, to have ideals rule. We are not always ready to "give our bodies with a man-sized will" to change our world and put ideals in power. We fail because we are tolerant, tolerant of right and wrong alike. We fail because we lack enthusiasm.

Consider the value Jesus set on the quality of enthusiasm. At a certain point in his ministry he beheld crowds coming to him in embarrassing multitudes. Half cynically he cried, "If any man cometh unto me, and hateth not his own father, and mother, and wife, and children, and brethren, and sisters, yea, and his own life also, he cannot be my disciple," lest they be low in enthusiasm. How he feared our obsessions with trifles that are always getting in the way of the serious business of life! A field, he suggested once, or a wife, or a yoke of oxen becomes for the moment more important than the Kingdom of God, the best. To cast back wistful glances at the tangible prizes given up for the sake of the best remained for him the one unpardonable sin. "He that putteth his hand to the plow and looketh back is not worthy of me," which literally means "can't be placed" in the Kingdom of God. The Master could not tolerate self-conscious, calculating sacrifice. We need truly "to take the brakes off our hearts" if we would be worthy of Him.

William James reminded us long ago of our inveterate habit of intensity. We are overcontracted personalities. Our temperaments have all the qualities of "bottled lightning." We pour into living an incommensurable amount of enthusiasm. Like violin strings long held taut, we are always snapping. But, alas, our intensity is spent upon trifles; our energy is wasted upon matters of no consequence. Diet, exercise, health, and investments get the ripe judgment and unremitting care that belongs to God, man, and our social well-being. Such enthusiasm as we have for the realm of the best is not unlike that vague cosmic emotion charged against one of our noble poets which consists in an undiscriminating "hurrah for the universe."

True, we enthuse over historic triumphs of moral right while at the same time we lack the social imagination to see their blood relatives in modern wrongs. Who that burns with indignation over the cruel Court of Spain which bred physical dwarfs for its own amusement, so pitiful in the paintings of Velasquez, sees the moral dwarfs bred by modern industrialism for our profit? Who that sympathizes with George Eliot's bitter line, "The Saints were cowards that they did not die, with Christ," sees new occasions for heroic living for Christ? Who that scoffs at the Pharisee thanking God that he is not like other men, "or even as this Publican," sees that it isn't the wrong things that we do, but the right things that we don't do that keep us out of the kingdom of heaven? "that we are damned not for doing wrong but for not doing right"? Verily, we too need a new baptism of enthusiasm, enthusiasm for the timely best.

In the shortest book of the Old Testament, the

shortest as it is the fiercest, the book of Obadiah, we witness a marshaling of invective that stings and burns beyond degree. The stinging phrases are pointed at Edom. The ancient prophet works his indignation up to a telling climax, a climax that is meant to be crushing: "In the day that thou stoodest aloof." Edom is the tribe whence sprang the line of Herod. Herod, the head of the line, sought the life of the infant Christ in his malicious slaughter of the innocents. Another of that line won the revealing title of Jesus, "that fox." That temperament, that moral perverseness traced back to a moral aloofness in the time of need. "In the day that thou stoodest aloof."

The struggle for excellence is again on. Our choice is clearly before us. With foxlike shrewdness we can make our way through life "minding the things of earth" as Paul so sadly says of some who had wrought with him, or with Christlike courage we can determine upon the things that are excellent for ourselves and our times. We have exhausted the catalogue of things that are excellent no more than the entrance examination exhausts the meaning and value of a college course. Let these things then stand for us as an entrance test: Humility, Courage, Loyalty, Enthusiasm. These are the things that are excellent.

# CHRISTIAN UNITY

As pastor, builder, and Christian statesman, toiling in behalf of the upbuilding and unity of the church, Dr. Ainslie has a unique place in American Christianity—as beloved as he is influential. A Virginian by birth, he was trained in the College of the Bible, Lexington, Kentucky, and entered the ministry of the Disciples of Christ in 1892, having found his field of labor before he was ordained.

For thirty-four years he has been a minister in Baltimore, where he has built up the Christian Temple, with which ten branch churches are associated; also the Seminary House for Bible Study and Neighborhood Betterment, which includes many beneficent activities. He is the President of the Association for the Promotion of Christian Unity, and the editor of its journal, *The Christian Union Quarterly.* In 1910 he was President of the National Convention of the Disciples of Christ.

Aside from books of devotion and exegesis—such as *Religion in Daily Doings, God and Me,* and more recently *The Way of Prayer,* the writings of Dr. Ainslie have been devoted largely to the cause of Christian unity. Besides his Yale lectures on *The Message of the Disciples,* are *The Unfinished Task of the Reformation* and, most striking of all, perhaps, *If Not a United Church—What?* So that the sermon following is one of the great themes of his life, alike in its simplicity, its directness, and its sweetness and earnestness of spirit.

# CHRISTIAN UNITY

PETER AINSLIE, D.D.

THE CHRISTIAN TEMPLE, BALTIMORE

*Till we all attain unto the unity of the faith.*

Ephesians 4: 13.

Here is a statement that has to do with an effort and a goal. Unity was not then and it is not now. Consequently it is something still to be attained. It is sure to come. It was the prayer of Jesus and the dream of Paul. It is written in the biology of mankind. A united Church is as fundamental in the program of Christianity as the death and resurrection of Jesus.

Whatever may have been its past, Christianity is destined to emerge from its centuries of entanglement into a world-wide social organism, with brotherhood as its cardinal principle, or it must decay. To apologize for the great chasms of unbrotherliness that exist among us today in consequence of our denominationalism is as though we were apologizing for present-day immorality. Instead of apologizing, we need an attitude of mind that will give expression to penitence and prayer. "Brother, for the sake of our Lord Jesus Christ, I beg of you all to drop these party-cries," was written by the Apostle Paul more than eighteen hundred years ago. It needs to be written again, and with pen of lightning, until the whole Church awakens to the need of setting itself to attaining unto the unity of the faith; for a denominational and divided Church cannot properly interpret the religion of Jesus. An institution that is at variance with itself is an incompetent agent to bear witness for a united world.

Whatever other factors there may be, there are certainly three that must function in any attempt toward unity. These are tolerance, equality, and fellowship. They have to do with the deepest experiences of life and can find expression only when guided by the spirit of Christ. In the history of Christianity, however, emphasis has so frequently been upon things of such far less consequence that these great realities have been obscured—sometimes so obscured as to be foreign to the prevailing experiences of Christianity; but the day has come when they are already discoverable in the evolutionary processes of Christianity toward its goal.

*Unity calls for tolerance.* It is sometimes maintained, and in some instances by learned men, that in tolerance there must be an uncertain or mild conviction, if not real indifference; but I dissent from any such interpretation. The fact is that intolerance is always an evidence of weakness and resorts to base methods to strengthen its weakness, whereas tolerance is the evidence of strength. Only the tolerant is sure in his convictions; hence he is not alarmed nor does he resort to base methods to establish them. He not only holds to the certainty of truth, but with equal fidelity to the worth of manhood. Both truth and man suffer when separated from each other. When attempts have been made to separate them, as has been done so often, we become involved in legalism, formalism, and unspiritual attitudes, which are destructive of faith and unity. Therefore there can be no fair study either of truth or of man apart from each other, held in the love of God as revealed in Jesus Christ our Lord.

It may be said that there are two equally abnormal and dangerous paths for one's thinking. One is that of intolerance, which leads to bigotry, if not to persecution. It has been a common path in the history of Christianity, reaching from the days of Constantine, through the centuries, by the fires of martyrdom, down to these days, when its remnant expresses itself in bigotry and ecclesiastical exclusiveness. The other has to do with "free thought," going headlong here and there, sometimes practicing an eclecticism that makes choices far and wide from the religions of the world, or adopts a skepticism that severely repudiates all religions, or mildly gives patronage to such as is suited to one's taste. However much church historians may give to the intolerant a place of preferment if his phrases were orthodox, and to the other a place outside the camp if his phrases were heretical, I do not hesitate to put them in the same group, for neither was the real interpreter of Jesus.

Over against these unspiritual divergences unity calls for tolerance, the normal and rightful path of which makes it possible for the soul to grow both toward others and toward God. Tolerance has to do with one's attitude of mind which lies back of all conduct. Toleration is the expression, but tolerance is that spirit of life that is an essential in the harmony of the universe. It is based on deep conviction of the truth and, at the same time, accords to others equal right to think regarding the same truth. It recognizes the greatness of God's mind and feels enriched to see the same truth from another angle. It advances only on the rising tide of spiritual life and seeks by reason to make the spiritual adjustment. It can flourish only in the atmosphere of a living faith and a wide vision. Denominational dogmas and party exclusiveness are destructive of tolerance. It lives by the way of Christ.

It does not figure on the discount of another person with whom there may be a difference of opinion or conviction; neither does it weaken in its conviction because another differs from it; but, in examining more thoroughly its own foundation, it endeavors to express in more reasonable terms an argument for the adjustment of the differences, always avoiding the separation of truth from personality. It does not deal in ultimatums nor anathemas. Those are the instruments of the weak. It forever recognizes its divine ownership and an equal ownership of all other souls. In tolerance the soul finds its way toward equality and fellowship.

*Unity calls for equality.* The denominational inequalities among Christians are as definitely marked as inequalities among races and in society. This inequality among Christians is based upon the arrogance of our theological interpretations, which, although not so severely proclaimed as formerly, nevertheless is very nearly as rigidly maintained with a sectarian remnant always pleading for the traditions of the fathers. These traditionalists belong to the Society of Samaria, of which the woman at the well was a lively exponent, saying, "Our fathers worshiped in this mountain and ye say that in Jerusalem is the place where men ought to worship." The whole denominational attitude, argument, and organization are out of date. The time for a united Church is overdue, and, to that end, there must be an equality of all Christians before God.

Our barriers of creed, episcopacy, baptism, or what not, are purely incidental by the side of the great principle of the equality of all Christians before God. If one wishes, he may have all these and more, so he practices Christian equality. If, on the other hand, holding to any one of these isolates him from other Christians, especially if there creeps into his thinking that, because he believes thus and so or has done thus and so, he is, therefore, better than other Christians; then that thing which he believes or which he has done becomes a hindrance to the will of God rather than a help, even though the Scriptures or the church councils may be cited for its authority. Many of the laws of Moses were altogether proper for observance in the time of Jesus, but there was scarcely anything against which Jesus more severely leveled his denunciations than the formalism into which those laws had passed.

It is precisely so in this day with the principles on which our Christian denominations rest. Whether they be Roman Catholic or Protestant, the motive for projecting them was good. Its purpose was to express truth and love. In passing out of an experience into a form it made denial of the great principles which are to guide Christianity into a united and spiritual brotherhood. Hence we are contending today with a form of truth which has largely become untruth and with a form of love which has largely become unlove, for anything that tends to separate the followers of Christ into non-coöperative camps is a false principle, irrespective of how it is labeled.

We must face the unchristian attitude of all these inequalities. One group of Christians, putting up barriers around the Lord's Table, the pulpit, and church membership and excluding other Christians and, therefore, proclaiming themselves better than other Christians, is an instance of sectarianism gone to seed. We must not be afraid to think our own way out of these instances of sectarian inequalities. Few could be found who would affirm that man's relation with God is dependent upon a certain creedal statement, or a certain form of episcopacy, or a certain form of baptism. We are beginning to observe that Christianity deals not so much with what as with whom. Our present need is to produce a Christianity that is near enough to the Christ that a non-Christian can easily observe that peculiar equality which Jesus set up for the world's standard, when he said, "One is your Master and all ye are brethren." That we are moving in the direction of that standard is heartening. The processes of development are breaking the crusts of pagan isolation and inequality. The practice of equality of all Christians before God means the releasing of new powers in the souls of the disciples of Jesus that shall hasten the unity of Christendom.

*Unity calls for fellowship.* Civilization has advanced by breaking down national isolations. It is so with Christianity. No denomination can maintain the policy of isolation, but its policy lowers the standard of Christianity and becomes a hindrance to the general growth of spirituality. We advance by maximums, not by minimums.

It has been said that on one occasion a British prime minister said in a speech before Parliament,

"Gentlemen, you must study larger maps." This needs to be said in every council of Christians, and said over and over again until all Christians come to understand that the boundary lines of Christianity include all who accept Jesus as Lord and Saviour. If there be any danger in drawing boundary lines, the greater danger is in exclusion rather than inclusion. Through the centuries, however, it has been the policy of the Church to confine itself largely to the study of small maps and, therefore, exclusions. In this lies the explanation of anathemas, divisions, and a world-wide denominationalism. It was the Greek Church putting the Roman Church under the ban and, in turn, the Roman Church putting the Greek Church under the ban. It was the Roman Church putting the Anglican Church under the ban and the Anglican Church putting the Nonconformists under the ban. It was the Roman Church putting the Protestants under the ban and the Protestants putting each other under the ban, until, all in all, there have been several hundred orders of excommunication, the monuments to which are seen in the several hundred divisions of Christendom.

It is usually claimed that such a course was necessary and we congratulate ourselves that these divisions conform to the laws of necessity, if not to the laws of God, when, as a matter of fact, it is not true at all. There is no law of necessity that could justify such a course, neither can any law of God be found that justifies it. The whole thing is wrong. Arguing from the biological principle of life, the first division of the Church was sin and every subsequent division has added to that sin, until today the greatest sin in the world is the broken fellowship of Christians. Fellowship must be restored, however great the cost, and this is our immediate task.

There are many indications of a world-wide awakening in Christian coöperation. America, Europe, Asia, Africa, and the islands of the sea furnish abundant illustrations. Denominational traditions, machineries, and policies may somewhat slacken these efforts, but they cannot turn them back. Christians of one group, in working side by side with Christians of another group in a common task, are discovering their common Christian kinship and their common Christian heritage. These discoveries have entered so deep into human experiences that to talk of blotting them out would be as absurd as attempting to blot out Columbus' discovery of America. Christian fellowship is growing around the world. Coöperation, acquaintance, and friendship are the experiences that lead to fellowship.

Fellowship is a spiritual experience. As that spiritual experience deepens, denominational barriers weaken before it. Its hunger reaches out to all Christians. Denominational lines grow more and more artificial and the reality of God in the soul becomes more evident. It is the normal attitude of the Christian. When fellowship was broken by a multiplicity of divisions in the Church, Christianity became an abnormal product; and it will remain so until it finds the path to tolerance, equality, and fellowship.

Cicero's accusation of Catiline is a parable for the times, and this time the interrogation is upon the lips of the Apostle Paul: O brother, how long will you abuse the patience of the Lord Jesus by continuing your party-cries? Has Christ been parceled out, part of him for one denomination and part of him for another and part of him still for another? Why do we continue to drown the voice of Jesus by our party-cries? An unsaved world is the price we are paying for our denominationalism.

Let us set our minds to attaining unto "the unity of the faith and to the knowledge of God's Son, reaching maturity, reaching the full measure of development, which belongs to the fullness of Christ—instead of remaining immature, blown from our course, and swayed by every passing wind of doctrine . . . for Christ is the head and under him, as the entire body is welded together and compacted by every joint with which it is supplied, the due activity of each part enables the Body to grow and build itself up in love." To him be glory forever. Amen.

# THE HUMAN HARVEST

Dr. Jones is a Virginian, born in the wake of the Civil War, the son of a famous chaplain in the southern army who was a biographer of Robert E. Lee; in fact a member of a family of great preachers, and so predestinated to the pulpit. Educated in the Washington and Lee University and at the Southern Baptist Theological Seminary, he was a graduate student at the University of Virginia after his ordination to the Baptist ministry in 1893. After brief pastorates in Kentucky, he went to the Leigh Street Church, Richmond, from which he was called to the First Church of Augusta, Georgia, where he spent nine happy years. Since 1917 he has been pastor of the Ponce de Leon Avenue Baptist Church, Atlanta, as well as a Director of the Inter-racial Commission, to which we owe so much advance in the direction of racial comity and coöperation in the South.

So far Dr. Jones had published little except his very interesting book entitled *Text and Pretext*, which, like the sermon here following, makes us wish he would give us more in the same manner. In the full ripeness of his splendid powers, of late years he has won wide fame, North as well as South, both as a preacher of distinction and charm and as a sagacious leader of Christian enterprise. By all rights we are entitled to a volume of his sermons, as all will agree after reading this exposition of the mission and method of Jesus: the faith of Fairyland which is also the faith of the Kingdom of God.

thing in men. Without that something, all that He could bring them would be useless.

We make music, believing that there is a sensitiveness to harmony in others which will respond to the appeal of the concord of sounds. We paint pictures, believing that there is in others an appreciation of beauty, which will answer to the appeal of beauty. So Jesus came calling to men, believing that there was that within human nature, which would vibrate to the divine voice. He believed that there was within every man a capacity to think His thoughts, to thrill with His sentiments, to be uplifted with His ideals, and to love with His passion. It was this deathless faith which held Him confident through every trial and temptation. "They will hear my voice. I, if I be lifted up," will attract that quality in human nature which is akin to the divine, and "I will draw all men unto me."

So, as He walked along the narrow streets of Capernaum, He saw, seated in his office, a tax-gatherer. The men all about Him saw in this man a traitor to every standard of patriotism. He was greedy, cold, and cruel, living like a vampire upon the lifeblood of his countrymen. Jesus saw all of this, and read its deadly significance with a far deeper interpretation than any of those who saw with the eyes of hatred. But He saw infinitely more. "Matthew, follow me." Something in Matthew awakened from its sleep. Something latent in his spirit stirred like a sleeping babe in answer to the call of the mother voice. That something responded, and there stepped forth, in answer to the Master's call, Matthew, the disciple, the loving biographer of our Lord.

They have dragged a woman, all soiled with the filth of her degrading sin, and thrown her at His feet for judgment. And now they stand circled in self-righteous superiority to test Him by His judgment. He sees all that they see, but, looking into the depth of her soul, with eyes of sympathetic love, He sees more. "Woman, go and sin no more." And, as she looked up in startled surprise, she looked, no doubt, for the first time into the eyes of a man who believed that she could "go and sin no more." In those eyes she sees a faith in her possible purity, and instantly there is the answering radiance of loyalty to meet His faith.

It is this belief that there is good in every life which gives Him His universal appeal. He believed that in every man, beneath the débris of broken promises and the wrecks of righteous resolutions, there are traced with the divine finger the plans and specifications of a man made in the image of God. And here, and here alone, is the reason for His universal gospel—His glad tidings to all men. All men are His children. They are unconscious of their relationship, and it is the Father-voice which is needed to awaken the sense of childhood. The "whosoever" invitation is not a divine mockery, nor a spectacular fiction. "Whosoever will" can come into a redeeming "consciousness of kinship" to God.

This view of human life is absolutely necessary before we can do the Christ work in the world. So long as we believe that human nature is inherently bad, our appeals will be to ignoble motives. Of course there is the capacity for the bad, as well as the good, in every man. There is a "worst" just as there is a "best." Which is to be realized in character depends so largely upon which is appealed to. When we call to the selfishness of men, selfishness responds. When we appeal to vanity, vanity answers. When we call to greed, greed is awakened. We must believe that there is a best in order to appeal to that best, with a passionate faith that it will respond. Only as we believe there is a divine kinship that will respond to a divine appeal, can we speak with the Master's voice.

Is not the Master's experience in the wilderness repeated in some form in the life of every man who seeks to serve? Just when one is about to challenge the discipleship of men to some great truth, dare their loyalty to some great enterprise, or call them into fellowship in some great movement for righteousness, there comes the whisper of a satanic voice: "You are pursuing the wrong method, you must be practical. Every man has his price. Human nature is selfish. You must appeal to selfish motives."

It is the old, satanic doctrine that this world belongs to the devil, and in order to win men, one must bow the knee to him. But Jesus is saying to us: "It is false. They are mine. Call them in my name, and in my spirit, and they will answer, for they know my voice."

This is not the faith of a dreamer or a sentimentalist. Neither is it the call to men to ignore the facts of life, or overlook the deadly danger of sin. It is the faith inherent in the moral law, itself, and grows out of the very nature of right and wrong. So far from it being an effort to minimize the deadly danger of unrighteousness, or to overlook the gravity of sin, it grows out of a deeper understanding of the nature of good and evil.

The very fact that a man can commit a wrong is evidence of his ability to do that which is good. Each sin which shocks our moral sense is a testimony to the truth that, within the life of the sinner, there is the possibility of righteousness. We condemn a man for stealing because we know he might have been honest. If he were compelled by his nature to steal, we would have the horrid revelation that there was no moral capacity in him. We hold the liar accountable for his lie, because he might have told the truth. The tongue which cursed could have been musical with blessing. The hand which curled into a fist with cruel blow, might have been tender with the healing touch of helpfulness. The eyes which blazed in cruel anger could have been radiant with the light of love.

Sin is always a failure. It is a failure to be one's best. So we cannot tell how great is the sin, until we know how great is the best. We cannot know the depth of the fall of a man, until we can measure it by the height of his possible attainment. It is only from this standpoint that we can come to understand the meaning of the word "lost," as used by Christ. It is not the man which *is* that is lost, but that best man which might have been. We might picture to ourselves today the most hopeless specimen of human life which we know; every trace of human kindness, sympathy, and nobility has been blotted out. Vice has written the ignoble story of its selfish greed and bestial indulgence upon every feature. The light has gone out of the eye, and the smile has faded from the lips. Debauched and degraded, there is naught left of that which we are wont to call human. This man, we are accustomed to say, is lost, and yet the man which we see is not the lost man. This body might be tossed aside into the waste and wreckage of human failure, and the world would be better for his going. No, it is what is not here, in this human form, which is lost. It is the man he might have been. One who knew him in his boyhood might recall the light of promise in his eyes, the vibrant tone of command in his voice, and the heroic bearing of his youthful figure and, remembering the hope which he stirred within the hearts of those who loved him, picture the man that he might have been. Yes, it is that man, pictured by the promise of the boy—that man which might have been—which is lost.

Here, then, is the explanation, not only of the mission, but of the method of Jesus. From this standpoint we can understand His saying, "I came not into the world to condemn the world, but I came to seek and to save that which is lost." No wonder the Pharisees, with their love of forms and ceremonials, and their mechanical conception of righteousness, were shocked at the manner of Jesus with men. "This man eateth and drinketh with publicans and sinners; he consorteth with harlots and outcasts of society." And nothing could have justified this unconventional conduct of the Christ in mingling with the mean and the low of society, save His faith that in each life, imprisoned or buried, there was a life worth saving, lost to men and God. And He believed that that lost man could only be reached by the voice of love and the challenge of faith. So He moved among men, calling to their best, and it was their best which responded.

It seems difficult for us to understand that if we are going to do the work of the Christ in the world we cannot do it without His love and His faith. How many of us remember the creed of fairyland? It is this—"One must be loved, to become lovable." Yes, it is this transforming power of love which works the miracles of character. One of the most exquisite of all the fairy stories runs something like this:

Once upon a time a princess was turned, by horrid magic, into a dragon. And then a good fairy—there are always good fairies—came to the King, her father, and told him that if he could find in all the land a valiant knight who would ride unafraid into the forest, and, without threat or weapon, walk up to the dragon and kiss it upon the lips, the spell would be broken. The King makes the proclamation and promises that if such a knight be found he shall be rewarded by the princess as his wife. Knight after knight makes the attempt, but each, as he faces the horrid visage of the revolting monster, turns back in disgusted failure. And then the hero-prince comes. Alighting from his horse, he walks straight into the depths of the forest, with never a hesitant step, and the smile upon his face never fails. With the memory of the beauty of the face of the Princess in vivid charm upon his mind he never sees the face of the dragon. Stepping forward to place his lips upon the lips of the beast, he touches the lips of the beauteous Princess.

This is the faith of fairyland, and this is the faith of the Kingdom of God. This is the magic of fairyland and this is the miracle of the Kingdom of Heaven. There is, in a real sense, a very beautiful personality lying latent within the animal life of every man. Only a love like that of the Christ can awaken it. And only those with the passion of the Christ can enter the comradeship of His service. We, too, are sent into the world "not to condemn," but "to seek and to save." Is not this the meaning of "the harvest field," and the need for "laborers"?

# A LAYMAN LOOKS AT RELIGION

A Missourian by birth, still on the sunny side of forty, Dr. Frank was educated in the Normal School in his native state, and at Northwestern University, where, in 1912, he became Assistant to the President. For three years he was associated with Edward A. Filene in research and organization work, doing a deal of lecturing the while with the Lyceum Association, until 1919, when he became associate editor of the *Century Magazine.*

In 1918-19 Dr. Frank was a member of a group, headed by former President Taft, that drafted a covenant for the League of Nations, which was considered by the Peace Conference at Paris. In the same year appeared his book *The Politics of Industry,* and also his study of *The League of Nations,* its principle and practice. As editor-in-chief of the *Century Magazine* since 1921, he has won a unique place as a publicist, making the *Century* not simply a journal of literature but a forum of constructive, forward-looking opinion. He has recently been elected President of the University of Wisconsin, a post of liberal leadership for which he is superbly fitted by temper, training, and genius.

The following sermon, in the manner of his volume, *An American Looks at His World,* is a searching survey of Protestantism and its tendency to disintegrate into sects—some of them small enough to be insects—in a world groping its way toward unity in a day when there is little "open vision" and no spiritual program. It is a voice from the pew, rebuking the angry debates of the hour, asking for the bread of life instead of a stony logic.

# A LAYMAN LOOKS AT RELIGION

GLENN FRANK

LATE EDITOR CENTURY MAGAZINE; PRESIDENT UNIVERSITY OF WISCONSIN

*By their fruits ye shall know them.* Matthew 7: 20.

American Protestantism is becoming self-conscious. I do not refer to the self-consciousness of those pre-adolescent Protestants who don their hoods and spend haunted hours worrying over some mythical menace of Catholicism. I refer rather to the self-consciousness that is being brought about by the current controversy in the Protestant churches between the literalists and the liberals, between the Fundamentalists and the Modernists.

Protestantism is cross-examining itself. It is beginning to ask itself where it is going. This cross-examination is no easy matter, because Protestantism is not a coherent religious movement. It is a medley of religious movements. It is a tangled mass of tendencies that differ as day differs from night. The Reformation did not create a unified something called Protestantism that can be isolated and studied as one may isolate and study Roman Catholicism, which is a unified and coherent thing.

As H. G. Wells has phrased it, the Reformation

detached great masses from the Catholic Church, set up a vast process of fragmentation among Christian associations, and drove large fissures through the then common platform of Christendom, with the result that today people are divided by forgotten points of difference, by sides taken by their predecessors in the sixteenth century, by mere sectarian names, and by the walls of separate meeting-places.

Protestantism is a protest that has not hung together. In speaking of Protestantism, one hardly knows whether to say "it" or "them." I am by temperament and by training a Protestant, but I am convinced that Protestantism must achieve an increasing unity or be content with a decreasing influence.

The extensive denominational division of American Protestantism is a travesty upon the religion of Jesus. The denominational divisions, by the very fact of their existence, are stumbling-blocks in the way of the spiritual effectiveness of Protestantism. It has long been said that denominations are necessary in order to satisfy different types and temperaments of human nature. But can any honest observer seriously contend that today our various denominations are each ministering to a distinct type or temperament of folk? Of course they are not. There are deep-going differences of human temperament that mean different approaches to religion, differences of temperament that may well require different kinds of churches. But these differences may, I think, be reduced to two in number. Humanity is rather clearly divided into two camps, those who like to have things done for them and those who like to do things for themselves. The difference between these two sorts of folk is so basic that to the end of time there will be folk who cannot find spiritual satisfaction save in a church of authority, and there will be other folk who cannot find spiritual satisfaction save in a church of liberty. The thousand and one other variations of temperament may, I think, be justifiably grouped under these two, the authoritarian temperament and the libertarian temperament. Obviously the existing Protestant denominations do not exist to serve any such basic differences.

Our Protestant denominations are very much like our political parties. They came into existence as champions of ideas and policies that had, or may have had, reality at the time, but most of the specific issues that called them into existence have been met or mankind has come to see that they were not as real as they seemed. So that our Protestant denominations, like our two major political parties, are the artificially animated ghosts of dead issues. Their separate existences are not justified by realities. There is as great variety of temperament and as great diversity of opinion within our political parties as between our political parties, within our denominations as between our denominations. They have outlived the reasons that called them into existence. They are held together by inertia, by pride of organization, and by the power, often the unconscious power, of vested interests. The various denominations of Protestantism are no more making unique or distinctive contributions to the advancement of religion than the Democratic and Republican parties are making unique or distinctive contributions to the advancement of good government. Religious denominationalism is to the spiritual future of the race what political nationalism is to the social future of the race, an obsolete conception standing in the way of that "moral and intellectual reunion of mankind" that is the old valid goal of history.

But when I speak of the imperative need for an increasing unity in Protestantism I do not mean what is commonly called "church unity." I mean a deeper unity of spirit and purpose. I have thrown in these observations on denominationalism as a sort of aside. So many discussions of "church unity" are couched solely in the political terms of ecclesiastical compromise and in the economic terms of the elimination of the waste of competing church plants! Frankly, I do not see that any great spiritual gain is likely to come as the result of a "church unity" that is brought about by the same sort of arguments that effect mergers of steel plants and cotton mills. Protestantism needs a unity that will come as the result of a new vision of itself and its purpose, as the result of a new spiritual and intellectual awakening. And nothing gives greater promise of a new and deeper unity of spirit and purpose than the self-conscious and self-questioning mood in which Protestantism now finds itself.

I want, if I can, to give something of a picture of this self-conscious mood of Protestantism. I do not know where Protestantism is going. Nobody knows. And I shall not, as a mere layman, presume to suggest where Protestantism should go. I shall content myself with the simpler task of trying to set down some of the questions that I think serious-minded Protestants are asking themselves. I shall not hesitate to express, for what it may be worth, a personal opinion on some of these questions, but my primary purpose is to try to take a sort of moving-picture of the mind, the unsettled mind, of Protestantism.

I suggest that, before Protestantism can achieve a greater unity of spirit and purpose, we Protestants must ask and answer such questions as these:

Shall Protestantism return to Rome, to Athens, or to Jerusalem?

Shall Protestantism be the religion of a church, the religion of a book, or the religion of a spirit?

Shall Protestantism be a religion of authority or a religion of adventure?

Shall Protestantism be a religion of magic for primitive minds or a religion of mysticism for modern minds?

Shall Protestantism be a religion of deliverance for the sick-minded or a religion of development for the healthy-minded?

Shall Protestantism be a religion of declarations or a religion of demonstrations?

Shall Protestantism be a personal religion or a social religion?

Shall Protestantism take its cue from the scientist or shall it take its cue from the mystic?

Now, these are not eight distinct questions. They could probably be boiled down to two or, at most, three questions. Careless of duplication, I have set them down in order to catch the various shadings and aspects of Protestantism's questioning mood. Let me try to suggest how, as it seems to me, these questions strike the average layman who is not a student of church history, of theology, or of the newer activities in the field of religious psychology.

For instance, the average Protestant layman has not made a profound or detailed study of the Roman, the Greek, and the Hebrew elements in contemporary Christianity. When he asks whether Protestantism should return to Rome, to Athens, or to Jerusalem, he doubtless oversimplifies the problem. To him I think Rome represents simply the tendency toward a vast and authoritative organization that standardizes belief and, save in the case of the exceptional mystic or saint, leaves little freedom for personal adventure and experimentation in religion.

To him I think Athens represents simply the Greek tendency toward metaphysical theology, toward great concern with doctrinal definitions, toward speculation. And to him I think Jerusalem represents whatever the original religion of Jesus seems to him to have been before either the organizing genius of Rome or the speculating genius of Greece got hold of it. And unless he is an ardent Fundamentalist, I think he would like to see Protestantism return to Jerusalem, not to stay there, not to attempt a slavishly literal reconstruction of every aspect of primitive Christianity, but to return to Jerusalem as one, lost in the woods, would like to get back to the starting-point of the journey in order to get one's bearings and direction afresh.

The intelligent layman knows, I think, that many aspects of primitive Christianity were rooted in and colored by the time and place of its origin. All such aspects plainly have no more than historical interest for modern men. I do not believe that the intelligent Protestant layman looks upon the religion of Jesus as a religion incapable of growth. Much, for instance, of what goes by the name of the "social gospel" has probably been read into the New Testament record by overzealous apostles of a "new social order." To me, at any rate, the New Testament record seems to portray Jesus as less the social engineer than many modern interpreters make him. But this fact seems to me in no way to invalidate the claims of the social gospel. The social gospel is a valid *development* of primitive Christianity. The germ of it was there. And every page of the record seems to me to suggest that were Jesus preaching in the synagogues, cathedrals, and chapels of modern America, or on the street corners to which he would probably be driven, he would be found in the ranks of those preaching the social gospel rather than in the ranks of those who restrict Christianity to metaphysical and otherworldly considerations. More and more laymen are, I think, feeling that there is a distinction between the religion of Jesus and theological Christianity. And they would, unless I misread their desires, like to see Protestantism return to Jerusalem, divest itself of the many accretions it has taken on as it has passed through Roman and Greek civilization, and thrust its dynamic into the life of modern America, there to create realistic and valid forms of thought and action that honestly express the modern American rather than the ancient Roman or the ancient Greek.

I think the average intelligent Protestant layman would like to see Protestantism become frankly and fully a religion of the spirit rather than the religion of either a church or a book. The Reformation denied the Catholic contention that pope and church must be looked to for the infallible interpretation of the Bible and doctrine, but retained the conception of the Bible as an infallible book to be interpreted by the private judgment of the individual worshiper. But of what use is an infallible book in the hands of fallible interpreters? The notion of an infallible book *and* an infallible interpreter cannot be split in two parts. It is either true or false as a whole. Every year I meet more laymen who feel that there is no halfway house between Roman Catholicism and whole-hearted Protestant Modernism. Those readers who have followed my earlier essays on the religious situation know that I do not feel that Modernism has yet found itself. It has far to go before it can satisfy "the soul of the saint" as well as "the intellect of the scholar." But with all my reservations, if I were not at heart a Protestant Modernist, I should be a Roman Catholic. The Protestantism of the old Reformation is, it seems to me, simply Roman Catholicism rendered illogical, Roman Catholicism with the keystone of its arch removed.

As William Pierson Merrill said in a recent issue of the *World's Work:*

> Protestantism is today in a critical position. It may have had its day, and henceforth exist as a declining, weakening cause. It may burst into new vigor, and go on into the splendor of a new day and a new life. Whether this or that shall be its destiny depends on Protestants themselves, . . . on whether they let their churches remain partly Catholic, or make them wholly Protestant. The danger does not lie in any "Roman peril," in any "Catholic encroachments," which Protestantism must stoutly resist, or be driven from the

field. The remedy does not lie in the use of propaganda, or any other outward means of defense or offense, whether the coarse indefensible methods of the Ku Klux Klan, or more subtle anti-Catholic agitation. The simple remedy is in making Protestantism true to itself. . . . Protestantism will be doomed to dwindle and die, if it keeps on trying to compete with Catholicism on its own lines. The Reformation went but part of the way.

We are not called upon to be swaggeringly dogmatic and irritatingly cocksure, but we are called upon to be consistent.

I think the average layman is pretty clear about the apparent competition between the notion of Christianity as a personal religion and the notion of Christianity as a social religion. He does not want Protestantism to be either exclusively; he wants it to be both. He dislikes to hear the terms "spiritual gospel" and "social gospel" used separately, as if Christianity were departmentalized, as if a man could say at one moment, "I will now be a spiritual being and exercise my soul," and the next moment say, "I will now be a socially minded citizen and work for the common good." Such a conception belies the essential unity of life; it is a travesty upon the coherent purpose of the religion of Jesus. I think the average intelligent layman feels that Protestantism owes it to civilization to effect a reconciliation of the party of "personal religion" and the party of "social religion." Unless we can socialize our religious program and spiritualize our social program, the influence of the church will decline in our national life, and our social development will degenerate into a selfish and purely materialistic struggle for class interests. As I have said before in these columns, the world does not need a church that is either a retreat for mystics alone or a reform club for radicals alone, but is waiting for a religious leadership that can talk economics so that men will feel in the presence of God.

And, again, Protestantism dare not become either a religion of deliverance for the sick-minded or a religion of development for the healthy-minded. It must be both, for there are both kinds of folk at the church doors. It is difficult to avoid letting the emphasis lie too much in one or the other direction.

I am not trying to answer questions in this sermon; I am trying rather to raise questions that I think Protestantism must answer. I have kept this a layman's discussion because he is the innocent bystander in much of the current controversy between the Fundamentalists and the Modernists. In these battles of doctrine the man in the pew feels that he is often strangely neglected. I think I know how most of the men in the pews feel about this controversy. I am one of them, and so I venture to speak for them.

We laymen are not greatly interested in the technicalities of theological discussion. We are interested in the mystery and the mastery of life. That is what religion means to us. We are neither pure scientists nor pure mystics. There is something of both in us. When we go to church we want light on the mystery of life and leadership in the mastery of life. And, frankly, we are getting little light and less leadership from the present theological warfare that is turning so many of our churches into debating clubs.

Some of us are Fundamentalists; some of us are Modernists. We may differ in our beliefs, but we agree in our desire. We want from the church spiritual leadership in the problems of life more than we want intellectual leadership in the problems of doctrine. We know that these two ministries are not wholly separate, but we want them mixed in the right proportions.

We laymen have seen theology become a mere intellectual chess game in the hands of Modernists as well as in the hands of Fundamentalists, and *vice versa.* And when this happens, we feel that there is little to choose between the two.

We want our religious leaders to study theology, but we want them to use the results of their study to give them a point of view from which to talk to us about the problems of life. We do not want a carpenter to give us his tools; we want him to use his tools to build us a house in which we can live, in which we can find protection, comfort, and refreshment that will fit us for our tasks. We shall starve if we are fed upon either metaphysics or negations. We are not interested in the roots of theology, but in the fruits of theology.

We are asking for the bread of life, but in the heat of this controversy we often get only the stone of logic.

# A SERMON IN STONES

As Beecher was wont to say, no one can understand the theology of the last century who does not know Swedenborg, whose serene and emancipating vision influenced thought and faith more than we realize, especially in respect of the future life and its conditions. In other ways, too, a small communion has been influential out of all proportion to its size. For that reason, as well as others, I am happy to have a sermon by a distinguished New-Churchman, as a gracious note in our pulpit symphony.

A Marylander by nativity, trained in the schools of his church, Dr. King has held three notable pastorates, the first in the Calvert Street Church of the New Jerusalem in Baltimore—the oldest New Church parish in America, having been organized in 1792. After more than a decade in Baltimore, he went in 1893 to the Church of the Divine Humanity in Chicago, where, at the end of ten years, his health gave way, and he sought recuperation in Lakewood, Ohio. Shortly after his arrival he began to hold services in a little chapel, which has now grown to be a large parish with a new edifice and a place of power in the community.

There is a quality of quiet beauty and penetrating insight in the sermon following, and withal a serenity and assurance which must make appeal in these hectic days when so many strive after cleverness and miss rich stores of symbolism and color, such as are revealed in a style of simplicity and charm in what I have ventured to describe as A Sermon in Stones.

# A SERMON IN STONES

THOMAS D. KING, D.D.

CHURCH OF THE REDEEMER (SWEDENBORGIAN)

LAKEWOOD, OHIO

*And the stones were according to the names of the children of Israel, twelve according to their names, like the engravings of a signet, every one with his name, according to the twelve tribes.* Exodus 39: 14.

Aaron was Israel's first high priest. He comes before us, in the Bible story, as a very important character, and the things recorded of him and his official dress must impress us as having something more than a mere literal significance. Look at him as he goes in to minister before the Lord! Next to his body, he wears a coat. Around this coat there is a belt of soft material. Over this inner coat, he wears a blue robe that reaches to his feet. To this blue robe there is attached the ephod, which is a blue vestlike garment which covers his chest.

Over this ephod there is placed the breastplate, which is made of a piece of rich cloth with interstices of gold. The cloth of which the breastplate is made is double, and is nine inches square. At each corner there is a ring of pure gold, which is attached to the shoulder piece of the ephod by a chain of wreathed gold, and to the girdle of the ephod by blue laces. The breastplate is foursquare, and Aaron wears it over his heart. It is never separated from the ephod. In this breastplate there are set four rows of precious stones, of three each. The precious stones are removable. When Aaron goes in to minister before the Lord, he places the twelve stones in the breastplate. Putting these stones in the breastplate is a part of the solemn service at the door of the tent of appointment. The *first* row contains a sardius, a topaz, and a carbuncle. The *second* row contains an emerald, a sapphire, and a diamond. The *third* row contains a ligure, an agate, and an amethyst. The *fourth* row contains a beryl, an onyx, and a jasper.

The sardius is of beautiful red, and sometimes of a flaming color. The topaz is of a yellow or flame color, sometimes tinged with green, emitting a most splendid external luster. The carbuncle resembles a burning coal. The emerald is of a beautiful green. The sapphire, after the diamond, is the most precious of gems and is of a fine azure or sky-blue color. The agate exhibits a variety of beautiful tints. The amethyst is a gem of violet color, and of dazzling luster. The beryl resembles the emerald in color, but is much superior in texture. The onyx has a whitish ground and is variegated with bands of white and brown, and is of a fine flinty texture. The jasper is a precious stone of a brownish tint and occasionally striped with black.

# A Sermon in Stones

These stones, arranged in four rows of three stones each, were set in Aaron's breastplate and were called the Urim and Thummim. Set in Aaron's breastplate, they were worn over his heart; and when he went in to inquire of the Lord, he was answered from heaven by means of light shining forth from the precious stones.

## I

Aaron himself, as high priest, was a type of the Lord Jesus Christ; for of our blessed Lord, in His all majestic Divine Humanity, it is written: "He is a high priest forever, after the order of Melchizedek." St. Paul says of Him: "He is our high priest, touched with the feeling of our infirmity." Standing thus as the representative of the Lord, the high priest of human souls, Aaron's garments become typical of all the truths of Divine wisdom by which the Lord approaches us in loving ministry to our spiritual needs. Here may be seen the very glory of the incarnation. It was God coming in and down to our life and revealing Himself to us in our flesh and blood. It was Aaron, clothed—the eternal Word, made flesh. And here He stands revealed in a form we can see, think of and approach.

II

Aaron not only represents the Lord, as high priest, of heaven and the church, but he represents that quality of spiritual life that makes of all true believers royal priests unto God. The New Testament tells us of the priesthood of believers. We read: "He hath made us kings and priests unto God and His Father." The Lord's divine goodness, dwelling in the heart of the Christian believer, is the priest of God in the soul. Goodness—the goodness of the divine love; the goodness that comes from God and fills the soul with peace and disposes the whole man to gentleness, kindness, and service—is the Lord's priest in man. This spiritual goodness of heart, which is the Lord's own tender goodness made over to all who turn their hearts upward to Him, is that supreme virtue by which man has living and vital union with the Lord. All other Christian virtues fill a subordinate place in the mind. As all the families of Israel were held in connection with Jehovah through Aaron, the high priest, so all the elements and graces of the Christian character are held intact and have communion with God and heaven through the goodness of the Divine love, which becomes central in the soul, as the high priest of the regenerate heart. So far, then, as this goodness has been sought, found, and received—really enthroned in the heart—we have a priest within: a quality of heart that opens the mind to the Lord and makes communion with Him possible at all times.

Do not lose the force of this teaching. For it means that no one shall stand between you and the Lord. Religion is a personal, an individual matter. It is the name by which is designated the spiritual relationship of your soul and mine, to the Lord. No human being shall stand between us and the source of life. In the Jewish age, the people approached God through the priesthood. That was because the time had not come for God to reveal Himself in the Divine Humanity. He could come to man, and man could come to Him, only through representative persons and objects; but the incarnation ended and abolished all such representatives. The infinite was humanized—the Word was made flesh—the shadow faded, and the reality—the full blaze and glory of the Godhead broke upon the world in Jesus Christ.

The rending of the veil of the temple, by which the Holy of Holies became visible, represented the removal of all that had stood between God and man. For now, God *in* Christ may be immediately approached. The human soul, in its *own* name and right, may lay open its need to the Lord and come boldly to the throne of the heavenly grace. No priest need now stand between God and the human soul. The priest is within the human heart, in the form of that *Goodness* which is from above, and ever leading to personal communion with the Father of lights.

## III

But the principle of good, by which man is conjoined to the Lord, must be clothed with truth. Here we see the significance of Aaron's garments. They are the symbols of those divine truths which clothe goodness and give it proper form and expression. As garments clothe the body, so truth clothes the mind. Hence, there is so much said about garments in the Lord's Word: "Awake! Awake! Put on thy strength, O Zion; put on thy beautiful garments, O Jerusalem." "The King's daughter is all glorious within; her clothing is of wrought gold. She shall be brought unto the King in a raiment of needlework." It is very natural for us to think that when we come into the other life we shall love to learn the truth: but listen, our love for learning the Lord's truth in the spiritual world will depend upon the affection we have had for it in the present life. Simply changing worlds will not change us. "In the place where the tree falleth, there shall it lie." There is nothing in the simple process of changing worlds that will have the effect of awakening in our hearts an interest in the truth that we spurn and neglect in this present life. Of course, those who die in a state of simple good life—who have not had, in this life, opportunities of learning the truth, will be taught the needed truth in the Intermediate World; but those who willfully neglect the truth here, will do the same there.

## IV

This brings us to a consideration of the particular truths represented by Aaron's garments. There were, as we have seen, three garments worn by Aaron. These were, first, the embroidered coat, which was worn next to his body; second, the robe of blue, which was worn over the embroidered coat; and third, the ephod, which was the outermost garment.

The innermost coat! Instantly we think of the inner, seamless coat which our Lord wore and which was not divided. The innermost coat of Aaron, like the seamless vesture of the Lord, symbolizes the innermost harmony of the divine truth, such as it is in its inmost character. Truth, as it is externalized and brought out and down to the plane of outward life, accommodates itself to the external states of men's minds; but truth in its inner essence is a whole, a harmonious expression of the divine love. Such truth we find only in the spiritual sense of the Lord's Word. Truth of this character is symbolized by our Lord when He says: "They that wear soft garments are in King's palaces."

These soft garments—truths of the very spirit of the Word, truths inner and glowing with the light of the throne, are presented to us in the spiritual sense of the Bible. There they may be seen, studied, and acquired. As our minds are clothed with the spiritual meaning of God's Word, our inner affections come into form and manifestation. They do not pass away, but are clothed and remain, opening the inner mind to God and receiving into themselves His pure unselfish life. Over this innermost garment Aaron wore a robe of blue that reached to his feet. The robe of blue, worn over the soft inner coat, is the symbol of spiritual truth presented to the mind in the form of doctrine—truth systematized, doctrine coming from the Lord's Word and presenting itself to the understanding as a thing of rational faith. This is Aaron's long blue robe. It is the robe of the intellect—the rational clothing of the understanding.

Aaron could not go in to minister before the Lord without this robe of blue. To the spiritual man every act of his life is a ministry unto the Lord; but it must be an intelligent ministry. The religious life has its truths and laws—how can we hope to grow in it unless we learn them, become intelligent in them, and adjust our life to them? Life must be guided by doctrine. Instruction there must be; and the priest is here to impart it; but the people must come to receive, and think about it and individually grow intelligent in it. The doctrines of the church are for all—a robe of spiritual truth for your mind and mine. The profoundest joy of my life consists in helping you to become wise in the teaching of the church. For how can you meet life's demands—life's problems—without a clear knowledge of the Lord's truth?

And this blue robe must reach to the feet. Think of what that means! It means that what the church teaches, its spiritual doctrines, are a garment of blue for the whole man, that religion—the teaching about God revealed in the Divine Manhood of Jesus Christ; the teaching about the Lord's Word and its commandments; the teaching about Redemption and the saving power of the Lord; the teaching about marriage, its divine sanctity and purpose as the seminary of the human race; the teaching about the domestic life and the equality of man and woman; the teaching about business and the application of the principles of honesty in conducting it; the teaching about recreations and amusements and the place they fill in life—it means that all this teaching shall be more than mere dogmas, going in one ear and out the other, but that all this teaching shall become a robe of blue for the understanding—things of deep intelligence that shall enrobe every phase of life and descend to the *feet* of daily life in the world. It means in other words that life is to be guided by spiritual thinking—by an intelligence that covers its whole body down to the *feet*.

Over the long blue robe there was placed the ephod, which reached from the shoulders to the waist. This was the outermost garment of the high priest, and was the holiest garment worn by Aaron. This garment represented religion in life and practice. Religion that is not of life passes away. There is an inner realm of thought, emotion, and imagination, and there is an outer realm of practice where thought, emotion, and imagination take their investiture of flesh and matter and pass into nature and history. In one we have them in their warmth and fusion, in the other we have them crystallized into fact. Aaron's ephod stands for the crystallization—the bringing out and down of the religious thoughts and emotions awakened by the Spirit of God in the soul. Daily life is the very highest expression of religion; for all true religion has relation to life. This is the ephod—the outermost garment of Aaron.

To the ephod there was attached the foursquare breastplate. Some very important elements of Christian life must be indicated by the foursquare breastplate—what are they? The foursquare breastplate stands for a human life that, in its motive and thought, squares itself with God—that recognizes that all that is really good and true comes from Him—that feels the duty of loving and serving Him, ever conscious of the divine obligation to shun, as sin, all that is contrary to His will.

But a life that squares itself with God must, at the

same time, square itself with man. So the foursquare breastplate stands for a daily life that is just and upright in its relation to other human lives. No man lives unto himself. He is related to the human souls around him. They have claims on him. No man ever undertook to go to heaven alone without freezing on the way. For religion is not only a right attitude toward God, but also a right attitude toward man. It has its manward side as well as its Godward side. If our life is square toward the Lord and square toward our brother man, we are wearing the breastplate of the high priest.

V

These two aspects of the religious life are further enforced by the fact that the breastplate was *double.* The man whose religion consists merely in song and prayer—in what he thinks is a glorification of God—but who neglects the altruistic side of religion, does not fulfill the command to make the breastplate *double.* Religion does not belong exclusively to the skies. It must have respect to earth as well as to heaven. The church that separates religion from life has no connection with week-day affairs, and in a short time finds itself standing alone in the midst of society with no more living relation with its business than the bones that slumber in a churchyard. The breastplate must be double. Religion must include faith, creed, song, and prayer, but it must also include the world and man and society and business. From this, we may easily see the spiritual reason for the command not to *detach* the breastplate from the ephod. It means that daily life—life in the home, the office, the counting-room, and the shop—life, wherever we may be called to live it, must not be detached from religion, nor religion from life.

VI

Now, in the high priest's breastplate there were placed the twelve precious stones in four rows of three each. The precious stones were so arranged in Aaron's breastplate that the six stones on the right side derived their peculiar luster from the warm red glow, and the six on the left side from the warm blue shade. The symbolism of this arrangement of the precious stones opens up a most practical lesson. The number twelve is of frequent mention in the Bible, and always denotes what is *full* and complete. There were twelve tribes of Israel, twelve disciples of the Lord, and twelve gates to the Holy City. This number, thus employed, denotes the fullness and completeness of the truths of the Word and Church and their perfect adaptation to all human needs. The Urim and Thummim, or precious stones in Aaron's breastplate, symbolize the fullness of truth in the literal sense of the Lord's Word; and the communication which Aaron had with heaven, by means of light shining upon the stones, represented the conjunction of the church with heaven by means of the literal sense of the Bible.

The power of the Bible, however, to open heaven and consociate with angels, is realized only when its truths are learned and impressed upon the life. The precious stones must be *set* in the breastplate of an open, frank, and righteous life. The Bible, covered with dust on our bookshelves, or used as an ornament for a center table—the Bible unread in our homes cannot connect us with the Lord and heaven. It must be used. Its truths must shine in our minds. We must put them into the breastplate of our life. In the setting of the stones, they were equally divided. Six were on the right side and six on the left of the breastplate. Do you see what this means? It means that life has two sides, that the mind has two departments—the will with its affections, and the understanding with its thoughts.

The truths of religion exist for these two sides of life—for these two departments of the mind. A religion that is all heart, all feeling, all emotion, that does no thinking, that does not concern itself with the truth, but whose aim is only to arouse the emotions, runs into fanaticism; and while such presentations of religion appeal to the unthinking class and are of rapid growth, so far as crowds may be said to be growth, yet such a religion is unstable and has to be got and got over and over again. On the other hand, a religion that is all head, that places all virtue in mere doctrines and the cultivation of the understanding, runs into a cold intellectualism and turns the church into a cold-storage plant—a place rather to be shunned than sought.

Now, that which the Lord, in the opening of the spiritual sense of the Word and the reëstablishment of the Apostolic Church, has made possible, is a religion that is for the heart and for the head—a religion which *feels,* but also *thinks,* a religion with precious stones on both sides of the breastplate. The stones on the right side of Aaron's breastplate derived their luster from the sardius, or ruby, and had a warm red glow. They represented the truths of the Word in their application to the will or heart, truths glowing with the divine love and alive with the feeling and emotion of heaven. The heart with its warm feeling and tender emotion has its place in the religious life. Indeed, the lack of this element is a serious fault in the life of our church. We need more heart in our service, in our religion, in our daily intercourse with men. I am not speaking of that wild emotionalism that expends itself in meaningless ejaculations—in shouts of praise and hallelujahs—but of an emotion that warms into life a noble purpose and that gives zeal and ardor to devotion and life: a *heart* religion, a religion felt as an experience in the soul—the life of God breathing through the heart and quickening our own life.

This is what the precious stones, with their warm red glow, on the right side of the breastplate, stand for. But religious feeling must be controlled by enlightened reason. The intellect has an equal place with the heart in the religious life. Life must be properly balanced. We must have truths of love, of feeling, on the right side of the breastplate; but we must also have truths of faith, truths that lay hold of the reason and stimulate rational thinking, on the left side of the breastplate. Thus the precious stones on the left side derived their luster from the warm *blue* shade. Red is the symbol of divine love as a passion filling and animating the heart. Blue is the symbol of a cooler love—of the truth filling the understanding and giving right direction to love. And so, beloved, you have been called to a religious life that has balance and intellectual poise. Let the goodness of God's love in your heart put on the dress of Aaron; let the breastplate be set with these precious stones of truth and your life will be sweet and pure. Amen.

# LIFE'S FOOLISH RIVALRIES

Dr. Jones is a Texan, born in 1876, educated at the Universities of Missouri and Kentucky, taking up the study of law, which he abandoned in 1901 to be ordained in the ministry of the Disciples of Christ. After a brief pastorate in Cleveland, he went to the First Christian Church of Bloomington, Illinois, where, in a ministry of fourteen years, he became widely known as one of the most gracious and attractive preachers of the country. For three years, 1917-19, he was the president of the International Convention of the Disciples, and in 1920 he became pastor of the Central Church of Detroit, where he quickly won his way to a place of command in a city of great preachers.

Some of us well remember his first books—*The Inner Circle*, in 1914, followed two years later by *The Wisdom of God's Fools*—and the joy of discovering a master of the art of preaching, who united an exquisite artistry in homiletics with a brooding beauty of style; aptness and range of illustration with richness of insight into the delicate laws and forces of the spiritual life. His story, *Fairhope: The Annals of a Country Church*, revealed another side of a many-sided man, while his later volumes of sermons, such as *Ornamented Orthodoxy* and *When Jesus Wrote on the Ground*, disclose a ripening of his unique power of spiritual vision and winsomeness of appeal.

A friendly critic has described Dr. Jones as "an eighteenth century preacher in a twentieth century church," which is far enough from the fact, save as it may suggest the scholar who is an authority on Dr. Johnson, and the gentleman courtly alike in mind and in manner. No man among us is in more sparkling contact with the ideals and issues of his age, whereof the present sermon bears witness, in its appeal for a right ordering of values.

## LIFE'S FOOLISH RIVALRIES

EDGAR DeWITT JONES, D.D.

CENTRAL CHRISTIAN CHURCH, DETROIT

*And they with one consent began to make excuse. The first said, I have bought . . . And another said, I have bought . . . And another said, I have married . . .*

Luke 14: 18, 19, 20.

A discriminating critic of the writings of Charles Dickens accounts for their popularity in part by the numerous descriptions of appetizing meals. Lo! the steaming puddings, the meats roasted to just the right turn, the delicious fruits, and the frosted cakes—no wonder Dickens is popular. The point made by this critic might apply with equal weight to the Bible. The flavor of hospitality permeates its pages. Bible characters, whether kings, peasants, sages, seers, or apostles, are seen many times as hosts and guests, and often at the family meal. Jesus Himself moves amid such scenes very much at home. Many of His parables were spoken at the table. He has been called the Greatest of Table Talkers. He was a guest, not only in the home of friends, but of enemies as well. As for His parables, a number of them have for theme some phase of feasting—the host, guests, food, and drink.

This vivid parable of the Great Supper, sometimes called "The Parable of the Slighted Invitation," has in application been restricted largely to revivalistic uses. I do not remember hearing a sermon on this passage save of that character. The Great Feast, we are informed, is the Gospel which God has provided for all mankind. The excuses are the subterfuges offered by men and women who refuse to accept Him. I recall some able sermons preached from this passage, sermons that were shot through with evangelistic fervor, and effective in moving men and women to own allegiance to Christ. Such use of this passage of Scripture is warranted and always will be, but the restriction to such an application is not. The issue at stake is larger than that of enlistment, large as that is. The thought in this parable, and the principles involved, concern life in its entirety. The parable bears upon the rivalries of life, and it is as fresh, suggestive, and timely for our own day as when it was spoken nearly nineteen hundred years ago.

The Great Supper represents the highest good, the noblest aspirations, the very crown of life. It is the "First Things" of the Sermon on the Mount, the "Best Gifts" of St. Paul in the First Corinthian Letter. It is the "Fruits of the Spirit" of Galatians the fifth chapter. Ponder the parable from this viewpoint. The feast for the spiritual man is prepared, and sumptuously at that. The opportunity to partake is freely extended. The high privilege is put within the reach of a great number. The servant of the host went out at supper time to say to those who were invited, "Come, for all things are now ready." Then follows an astonishing procedure. "They all with one consent began to make excuse." What amazing stupidity! What strange indifference to the things that mean the most, that last the longest, and give the completest satisfaction! Three excuses are given and they are, so to speak, representative of the hundreds of excuses that might be offered, and indeed are offered constantly in refusing to accept the supremest of gifts.

The first refusal was based on the ground of newly acquired possessions. The man said: "I have bought a field." That settled it, he had bought a field, mind you. He had bought a piece of land—that was the overtowering event and hindered his attending the feast. He must look after that field; he must investigate the fences and examine the soil. How multitudinous the people who permit possessions to possess them! Instead of being the masters of what they own, they are the servants. The relation of property to personality is one of the most vexatious and difficult of problems. From the time that men struggled for existence and acquired property either by purchase or by conquest, property has been in one way or other a main issue of life. If Christianity teaches any one thing that is clear as a sunbeam, it is that life is more important than property; but society has not yet accepted that teaching. Ninety-five per cent of the laws on the statute books, both state and national, are for the safeguarding of property, and five per cent for the protection of life. As long as the bulk of the property is held by a few people, and the vast majority possess very little or nothing at all, the realization of a Christian community is difficult if not impossible. The peril of possessions and the abuse of property has brought about the two extremes that are inevitable under such conditions, to wit: those who hold the right of property as something Divine, and are jealous of any attempt to modify or weaken property rights; those who regard property as a crime and who would make private ownership either difficult or impossible by delegating to the State the power to confiscate all property for the general good. Christianity teaches, not the abolition of property, but the right use of property. It teaches that God is the owner and man the trustee. It is hazardous to put property above every other interest, and that is precisely what the man in this parable did. "I have bought a field," he said; "therefore I cannot come." As if that ended the matter for all time.

The second man declined the invitation to the Greatest of Suppers on the ground of commerce and a certain transaction in trading which he had recently consummated. He said: "I have bought five yoke of oxen and I go to prove them. I pray thee have me excused." Observe that the same phrase is used, the same metallic, cold, commercial phrase—"*I have bought.*" Terrible indeed is any kind of traffic, whether in live stock, clothing, stocks, bonds, or real estate, that dulls the finer instincts and crushes and kills the tenderer and more compassionate feelings. The ancient trader was an exploiter, and sometimes his modern successor is no better. Commerce and industry have their grimy and sordid side. The competitive system under which we operate is hard on both employer and employee. If the most of life is to be taken up with the tyranny of sale and purchase, of buying and selling on a cold mercenary basis, with much of "take" and but little "give," society cannot hope to reach the high level of Christ's teachings. America lost seventy-five thousand men during the nineteen months of our participation in the World War, yet during the same period two hundred and twenty-six thousand men, women, and children were killed accidentally in America. The larger part of these accidental deaths occurred in mines, factories, and other places of employment where the hazard was great or there was neglect of proper safety devices. Sixteen countries have eight-hour laws applicable to most industries, but ours is not on that list. Twenty-one lands plan special safeguard about mothers before and after childbirth, but ours is not recorded among them. Nearly every industrial nation forbids the employment of children in factories under fifteen, but Roumania, India, Spain, China and the *United States of America* are among the lands not yet on that high Christian plane. Signs are not wanting of a better day. Coöperation must replace competition everywhere; the frightful warfare between owner and worker cannot continue indefinitely.

The third man asked to be excused from attendance at the Great Supper on the ground of domestic obligations. He said, "I have married a wife and therefore I cannot come." This is in some respects the most extraordinary and unreasonable of the three excuses. The family is older than the church. God set "the solitary in families" long before the tabernacle was set up in the wilderness, the Temple erected in Jerusalem, or the Church was born on the day of Pentecost. To refuse to participate in the Greatest of Feasts on the ground that domestic duties hinder is the height of stupidity. Yet, all over this and other lands there are families who have postponed the culture of the finer things until it was too late. Interest is manifest in business, in society, in sport, in everything but a genuine devotion and loyalty to the things of the Spirit. To urge as a reason for declining to share in Spiritual riches the claim that there are prior obligations of a family nature is as though a flower refused to receive the light of the sun, arguing that its roots must first reach down into the soil. Is anything too good for the home? The best books, the best music, the best pictures, the best magazines—these are none too good for the place where little children are taught and molded for all time.

I remember once examining the nest of a robin. It was a most interesting home that robin had builded. There was a piece of fine lace in that nest; there were several yards of silk thread in that nest; there was a piece of dainty cambric, strands of tissue paper, and the stoutest of smooth straws most artistically woven into that nest. The birds had selected the best they could find and it was not too good. Many an American home might learn a lesson from that robin's nest. Cheap music, cheap jazz music, cheap magazines, shallow and sometimes indecent books, unworthy ideals—these do not belong in the home, of all places. The man who made the excuse that he could not attend the great supper because he was married was deluded or just a plain fool. The fact that he had "married a wife" was an extra good reason for his acceptance. *The tragedy of the parable is the treating of business, riches, and family duties as rivals or competitors.*

Truism that it is, let it be said again and again that religion is not something separate and aside from life. It is a mistake to speak of the soul of man as something apart from the man. It is time to discount such foolish talk as "saving one's soul and losing one's life." Religion, if it be anything, must be related to everything. Too many people get the idea that religion has to do mostly with singing, public praying, listening to sermons, and that a church building is "a religion container." We shall never be saved from the peril of property unless we are willing to use property in the light of the teachings of Jesus. We shall not know how to trade without peril to ourselves and to others except we trade in the Spirit of Christ and in the light of the thirteenth chapter of First Corinthians. And how shall we be able to build homes and rear families except by recognizing God in the family life and exalting the teachings of His Son? In a single generation, Germany's youth was molded for militarism by keeping before young life the warlike portrait of the militant Kaiser. Who knows what a generation might accomplish that was schooled in such a way of life as Jesus taught in His washing His disciples' feet in the Upper Room in Jerusalem?

The foolish rivalries of life lead us to vain attempts to live in apartments and divide life up into segments, labeling one part "Business," another "Pleasure," still another "Sport," and yet another "Religion." When the great invitation came to the men in the parable, there should have been no rivalry between the field, the oxen, the wife, and the Highest Good, the spiritual feast, the holiest of fellowships. The first man, had he been wise, would have said in response to the invitation: "I have bought a field, and therefore I am the more anxious to attend this feast. I must learn how to make the best possible use of this property which I have acquired." The second man should have reasoned: "I have bought five yoke of oxen; they probably will try me sorely before I have them broken to work; the probabilities are that I may be tempted to profanity. I need to go to this great supper in order to learn how to deal with those oxen, how to treat them as I should, and how to conduct my trading in such a way as not to betray truth, or honor, or take any undue advantage of a would-be purchaser." The third man should have reasoned similarly: "I have just married a wife and I am keen to accept the invitation. I propose to take her with me; we have started out on a long journey together. She may have a sharp tongue, and I know I have a beast of a temper. Most certainly we shall go to the Feast."

Travelers passing across the Mohave Desert observe with interest the long stretches of sand and sagebrush, drab and dreary—and then a moving picture, sharp by way of contrast, of a little station along the railway surrounded by a patch of the greenest of grass and set off with flaming geraniums. Why the great difference? *Water!* It is *water* that makes possible that greenest of grass and reddest of flowers. The miracle of irrigation is the explanation. The wilderness blossoms as the rose wherever the life-giving water is brought to lave its dry and heated bosom. Those stretches of desert where little of life exists but in reptilian form, those simmering wastes of alkali and sagebrush become a land of fruit and flowers and vegetables, and laughter and homes, wherever the streams of water come to bless. So too it is, that the world of business and industry and pleasure, so often cold and heartless and cruel; the world which crowns sometimes as victor those who do not deserve the prize, and in which defeat crushes and kills sometimes those who merit the highest reward; that world which is so often heartless to the core, flippant, sensual, and devilish—that selfsame world becomes just, righteous, kindly, tender, compassionate, beautiful, and friendly when the streams that flow from the fountain of heavenly grace flood the lives of men and women, and fructify the mind and affections in ways as wondrous as they are fruitful.

"Seek ye first his Kingdom, and his righteousness; and all these things shall be added unto you." That is to say, "these things"—food, drink, clothing, shelter—are *"added"* things. They are actually secondary things, yet they are important, and in their own way, essential things. The individual, family, community, nation, world that puts first things first will experience no rivalries and know no defeats!

# THE CONQUERING MIGHT OF WEAKNESS

Judged by any test, Dr. Aked is one of the outstanding preachers of his generation, uniting solid qualities of scholarly exposition with the most attractive powers of popular appeal. Yet, as is often true of great preachers, much as one enjoys his writings, there is something in him uncapturable in print, so that his books do not convey the full force and charm of his personality, much less his extraordinary gift of electrifying eloquence.

Born in Nottingham, England, Dr. Aked was educated in the Midland Baptist College and the University College of his native city. From the Pembroke Chapel, Liverpool, he came in 1907 to the Fifth Avenue Baptist Church, New York City —later named the Park Avenue Church, and now to be known as the Morningside Church. After four fruitful years a break in his health sent him to the West, where he became pastor of the First Congregational Church of San Francisco. Later he spent four years with the First Church of Kansas City, and now he has just returned to the Pacific coast, to the Wilshire Boulevard Church of Los Angeles.

Of the many books by Dr. Aked, the first to make him known in America was *The Courage of the Coward,* in which one may study his art, his insight, his method of approach. But some of us love best his expositions of *The Lord's Prayer* and *The Divine Drama of Job,* wishing the while that he would give us a volume of his Shakespeare interpretations. The sermon here following, by one who has known much of ill health, is a message of courage and cheer, as well as of faith and fortitude.

# THE CONQUERING MIGHT OF WEAKNESS

C. F. AKED, D.D., LL.D.

WILSHIRE BOULEVARD CONGREGATIONAL CHURCH, LOS ANGELES

*Power is made perfect in weakness.* II Corinthians 12: 9.

Some day, perhaps, we shall have an English version of the Scriptures in which the translators allow the Bible writers to speak for themselves. At present their interferences are innumerable. A favorite device is to insert in a sentence a word for which there is no equivalent in the original, the insertion of which, the translators think, will enable you to understand the sentence better. This addition, they believe, is warranted by the sense of the sentence they are translating; but, recognizing that their only authority for it is their own judgment, they print the interpolation in italics, warning you beforehand that you are to understand by the change of type that the word is no part of the original record, but a suggestion made to help you, which you are at liberty to accept or reject as you choose. This is perfectly fair, only, in reading the Bible, you forget all about the warning, ignore the change of type, and read the word as though it were an integral part of Holy Writ. Then you quote as "Bible" what is not

"Bible" at all, and feel quite a shock when you are pulled up and asked to listen to the original speech again.

"My power is made perfect in weakness," you read, and the "my" refers back to Almighty God. The word "my" must go out. It is printed in italics. Paul did not say it. He did not mean it. The translators think that it helps us to understand Paul. We misunderstand him if we accept their view. "My grace is sufficient for you," the apostle represents God as saying to him, "for power is made perfect in weakness"—not "my power," not the power of God, but Paul's own power, yours, mine, the power of anybody who, being weak and knowing his weakness, will put himself within the conditions of receiving strength—power is made perfect in weakness. It is a great word. Power is in the sound of it. There is something in the very syllables that make up the sentence which breathes vigor upon the soul. "Power is made perfect in weakness"—there are fightings in it and victories, and the rush of mountain winds and man's unconquerable mind. Is there one of us who has not loved strength and longed for it? Is there one of us that has not known weakness? Here is God's message for you, winged with flame and glory: "Power is made perfect in weakness."

Of course, the speaker is Paul. Who should it be but the heroic man whose frail body served the purpose of a death-defying spirit which turned the stream of history from its course and flung open the gates of morning to mankind? He knew; he had good cause to know; he had suffered too deeply, triumphed too sublimely, not to know that power is made perfect in weakness. And what that man did suffer, and what he accomplished in spite of his sufferings, or, as he would tell you, in consequence of his sufferings, is one of the marvels of the life-story of man upon this planet. Talk about miracles—the feeding of the five thousand and the raising of Lazarus from the dead—these are not worthy to be compared with the miracle of Paul. It is easy to recite his own clear-cut phrases which summarize the perils he braved and the persecutions he endured: "In labours more abundant, in stripes above measure, in prisons more frequent, in deaths oft. Of the Jews five times received I forty stripes save one. Thrice was I beaten with rods, once was I stoned, thrice I suffered shipwreck, a night and a day I have been in the deep; in journeyings often, in perils of waters, in perils of robbers, in perils by my own countrymen, in perils from the Gentiles, in perils in the city, in perils in the wilderness, in perils in the sea, in perils among false brethren; in labour and travail, in watchings often, in hunger and thirst, in fastings often, in cold and nakedness."

But we need to arrest the flow of words for a moment in which to realize the meaning of a single one of them. "Once was I stoned"; the stones are grasped with both hands, lifted above the head, flung one after the other upon the victim. Soon there is not a part of the body which is not bruised, hardly a bone which is not broken, the skull is fractured and bleeding, the nerves cease to quiver—the wretched man is left for dead! "Of the Jews five times I received forty stripes save one," the punishment of the ecclesiastical court; "thrice was I beaten with rods," the torture that the State inflicted. Often at the fifth blow the blood would begin to flow; when the fifteenth fell the flesh was one dreadful wound; before the thirtieth was reached the man was dead. The apostle endured, and added on to these agonies hunger and cold, heat and thirst, shipwreck and a thousand dangers and disasters by land and sea.

And this was a man of weak body and impaired health—possibly an epileptic. There was something physically repulsive in the ailment from which he suffered, so he says himself in his letter to the Galatians. He was racked by pain. He compared it to the torture of impalement. He speaks of it as "a stake in the flesh." Three times he sent up to God a cry for deliverance. But the sickness and the pain remained. So afflicted, he had to meet the fierce cruelty of that racial and religious hatred which has raged amongst the peoples of the countries in Asia Minor wherein he preached and labored, from the days when the Jew and the Canaanite devoted themselves to mutual slaughter to the hour in which the

Turk sought to tear up Christianity by the roots and wash it off the face of the earth in the blood of the Armenian people. And my friend, Dr. Deismann, writes: "And now we see this man, feeble in health, brutally ill-treated, brought down by hunger and perhaps by fever, nevertheless completing a life work that as a mere physical performance challenges our admiration." And this theologian, who is an archeologist and a traveler, and who knows the Anatolian country which was Paul's as he knows his own, constructs out of the memory of his own journeys a vivid sketch of Paul in that far-off day. He suggests that one try the experiment of going over the routes which Paul followed. He says:

With special passport and diplomatic recommendations in your pocket you have taken your seat in the comfortable up-to-date carriage of the Anatolian Railway, and in the evening twilight you are running on a track that engineering skill and dynamite have forced to pierce the rocks and cross the streams, towards the destination where your coming has already been announced by telegraph. As the train carries you without exertion over the top of the pass the last gleam of daylight shows you far below the ancient road, narrow and stony, climbing its way up the pass, and on this road a few people on foot or on donkeys, or at best on horseback, are hurrying towards the poor-looking dirty inn. It must be reached before night has fallen, for the night is no man's friend; the wild dogs kept by the rough shepherds bar the way furiously; robbers have designs on cloak and steed, and the dæmons of fever threaten the tired and overheated traveller in the cold night air that is already beginning to blow down the side valleys. Or, leaving the modern Levant hotel with its lift and French menu, go into the miserable khan on the top of the pass known as the Syrian Gates on the road to Antioch, and sleep for a single night on the hard boards of its unsavoury plank-beds, tortured by bad air, cold, and vermin. Or sail towards Italy from the east on one of the big Mediterranean steamers of the North German Lloyd; the storm that tosses you up and down in the dark night, and perhaps makes you a little seasick, cannot turn the mighty vessel from her course, but the little sailing ship, with no stars and no compass to guide her, is the plaything of the waves, and is thrown by the storm on reef or sandbank, and the few survivors drift about for days on fragments of the wreck, enduring agonies of hunger and thirst. On that darkening road we have seen St. Paul; on those hard boards Paul sought repose when weary; and it was Paul who drifted backwards and forwards on that ship's plank, a night and a day—Paul, the man who suffered so much from sickness. On my two journeys in Anatolia in 1906 and 1909 I had the great happiness and privilege of going over almost all the routes traversed by St. Paul; one of the most lasting impressions derived from these journeys, which were mostly made with modern means of locomotion, is my unspeakable amazement at the purely physical accomplishments of St. Paul, the traveller, who truly might say, not without reason, that he buffeted his body and brought it into subjection like a slave.

And our learned traveler adds to his vivid sketch Paul's own so mighty words: "Power is made perfect in weakness!"

There it is—the marvel that the frail body can endure so much, and, enduring, achieve the impossible! There is one surprise in the life of a physician which he early learns must not surprise him. "Which of us," a surgeon says in an address to his professional brethren, "which of us does not know patients who have lived for twenty years with an incurable disease; and which of us has not seen in the course of an autopsy organs so reduced in size and so altered in structure that it is incomprehensible how life was maintained?" Yes, indeed! For amongst ourselves it has become such a commonplace as to be almost a joke. My dear dead friend, John Watson, by virtue of the wise humor that was in him, insisted upon making a joke of it. When I myself lay sick and useless he undertook to cheer me by writing to me—you will find the letters in Robertson Nicoll's *Life of Ian Maclaren*—concerning the strange adventures of preachers who had lived with only one lung each—and lived to such an age that their congregations began to despair of ever seeing the end of them!

One of them [wrote Dr. Watson], quite a distinguished person, lived so long that he became a terror to a congregation from which he drew a retiring allowance, because he not only had a colleague, but that colleague grew old, and a third man was needed; and it seemed as if there was going to be a geological formation of colleagues, one upon the other, and all resting on the old red sandstone of this gentleman, aged ninety, who from the age of twenty-five had only possessed one lung.

And so on, until my friend came to the story of another who was a great preacher with a mighty voice and did so well with one lung that if he had had two his congregation might have sat in their own homes and heard him distinctly.

To be sure it is a commonplace, a commonplace of every day, but a commonplace at which every day we marvel, and for the marvel of which we have but the feeble words, "How can so frail a body do things so great!" None of us desires to be sick, and it would be very wrong of us to get into a mood so morbid that we were not anxious to fight disease wherever we find it. Preventable evils ought to be prevented. Yet we know very well that if the records of the world's great sufferers should be destroyed we should lose some of the brightest pages in all the history of humanity upon this earth. The entire conception of heroism has been raised for all time and for all the race by those "brave poor things" who have made the sick-bed a mount of transfiguration and proved that the frail and pain-racked body may yet be a temple of the Holy Ghost. Health is a blessing, and we all know it; and the doctrine of saving health is a good doctrine and true, for health "saves." But where amongst the young giants of the gymnasium and football field, "feeling their biceps and thumping their chests and thanking God that there is not a morbid fiber in their body," will you find the lives of blended sweetness and splendor which the records of sickness show? It is a simple matter of history that some of the noblest lives which have been lived on earth have been those of chronic invalids who have made their agonies a triumph and conquered all deadly things with Paul's word of life: "Power is made perfect in weakness."

We cherish the memory of Robert Louis Stevenson. Give me the pleasure of reading to you again a paragraph from his letter to George Meredith, from Samoa, in 1893:

> For fourteen years I have not had a day's real health; I have awakened sick and gone to bed weary; and I have done my work unflinchingly. I have written in bed, and written out of it, written in hæmorrhages, written in sickness, written torn by coughing, written when my head swam for weakness; and for so long, it seems to me I have won my wager and recovered my glove. I am better now, have been rightly speaking since first I came to the Pacific; and still, few are the days when I am not in some physical distress. And the battle goes on—ill or well, is a trifle: so as it goes. I was made for a contest, and the Powers have so willed that my battlefield should be this dingy, inglorious one of the bed and the physic bottle. At least I have not failed, but I would have preferred a place of trumpeting and the open air over my head.

And a greater than Stevenson—do you remember Goethe in his old age?

> I will say nothing against the course of my existence. But at the bottom it has been nothing but pain and burden, and

## C. F. Aked, D.D., LL.D.

I can affirm that during the whole of my seventy-five years I have not had four weeks of genuine well-being. It is but the perpetual rolling down of a rock that must be raised up again forever.

The story of Elizabeth Barrett Browning, like the story of the Brontë sisters, will be dear to all gentle souls as long as we read books and delight in them. Elizabeth Barrett Browning was, in our common phrase, "a martyr to ill health." But when was ever martyr of finer spirit than hers? In early life she was hurt by a fall from a horse. Her spine was injured. Her lungs were affected. She suffered from hemorrhage. Until she married she was kept prisoner by an insane father, and until she died was an invalid. Her father positively gloated over invalidism and all its morbid surroundings. She breathed an atmosphere of night and death. But the fiery brain burned on—and its flames still leap from her ashes. She had her Greek authors bound to look like novels for fear her physician should forbid continuous study; and, propped up on her couch by cushions, she wrote with a pencil on slips of paper—all her white, feeble hands could hold—works that the world will never let die.

The romance of the Brontë girls—Charlotte, Emily, Anne—consists in the absence of every romantic element! It is divinity draped in drab. Bad food and cruelty at school killed Maria and Elizabeth. Then Emily died at thirty years of age and Anne at twenty-nine. And Charlotte lived to early middle age, her starved soul claiming its birthright ever, and ever waging its victorious conflict with sickness and weakness, with poverty and discouragement and failure, with cramped and sordid surroundings, with the shadow and the sadness of mortality. Two things these enemies could not starve nor tame —the weird imagination that conceived *Jane Eyre* and the deathless courage which forced it upon a publisher and so upon the grateful heart of two generations of the English people. But the pathos of it—oh, the sadness of it! Yet Anne at least has shown us that she knew where consolation could be found. There is heartbreak in her words, but the light of the Resurrection morning is not far away:

I hoped that with the brave and strong,
  My portioned task might lie;
To toil amid the busy throng,
  With purpose pure and high;
But God has fixed another part,
  And He has fixed it well;
I said so with my breaking heart,
  When first this trouble fell.

These weary hours will not be lost,
  These days of misery,
These nights of darkness, anguish-tossed,
  Can I but turn to Thee:

With secret labour to sustain
  In patience every blow,
To gather fortitude from pain,
  And holiness from woe.

If Thou shouldst bring me back to life,
  More humble I should be,
More wise, more strengthened for the strife,
  More apt to lean on Thee:
Should death be standing at the gate,
  Thus should I keep my vow;
But, Lord! whatever be my fate,
  O let me serve Thee now!

Being dead she yet speaketh. They all speak to us—the Stevensons, the Goethes, the Brownings, the Brontës of this world and a countless host of strong sufferers who from the bed of pain—what one of them called "a mattress grave"—tell us that neither cold nor hunger nor poverty nor want nor chronic sickness with its fiery darts of pain and long lingering weakness, nor the living death of dying which is long delayed, can stay the spirit's flight to God nor quench its immortality. They know, these heroic sufferers, they know what Paul knew: Power is made perfect in weakness.

But why? These things lie on the surface. Such facts are known to everybody, though it is helpful to be reminded of them and to have them set in the light of religion. But can we go a little deeper into the problems that the phenomena present? The "why" is insistent. Power is made perfect in weakness. Why? What is the most constant characteristic of this condition of physical frailty which we have been discussing? Dis-ease, shall we call it—the absence of ease? No; let us say, rather, an exaggerated sensitiveness. When we are sick we are sensitive, often terribly, unbearably sensitive, to impressions which, in health, would not be impressions at all. A sound which we should not even hear when we are well becomes an intolerable irritation. A weight which we should not even be able to recognize as present becomes an intolerable burden; and the nerves are inflamed to the highest degree of sensitiveness, so that a touch is felt as a blow and a prick as a deadly wound. And it works both ways. Small kindnesses seem world-great when we receive them in our hypersensitive condition. Flowers represent a wealth of love; a look or a smile calls down heaven into the waiting heart.

There is another thing to be borne in mind as we try to understand the familiar fact which the apostle states. When we are denied the resources open to the normal person in normal health we turn to others. It is inevitable. If the things in which the robust person finds occupation are no longer for us, then in the hours of enforced idleness, the mind, soul, spirit—call it what you will—the intangible part of us which is the real You, the real I, turns to facts and forces up to that time forgotten or ignored. Remember that we have already agreed that at such a time we are immeasurably more sensitive to impressions, physical and emotional, our nerves alive with feeling. No wonder, then, that in such hours, or, it may be, years, the presence and the pressure of God are more immediately and more keenly felt.

You know how it is with the blind. You know that a blind person develops a sensitiveness of touch and of sound beyond all belief prior to demonstration. That is not all. A popular writer has written an interesting collection of detective stories, their hero a blind man.

The facts had to be told to him—the outer, visible facts; and then he sat in the darkness—seeing things, seeing them with that inner eye which is the compensatory gift to the blind. His mind was not distracted by the sight of the world around him. The world which exists for you and me, for him did not exist. From it he was shut out. He was shut up within himself. And induction with him became facile, while intuition amounted almost to divination. In one word, he "sensed" the facts that others could not find by sight. And it is not strange that when Frances Ridley Havergal first encountered the poems of Fanny Crosby, and asked who this dainty writer could be, she was told: "She is a blind woman in America whose heart can see splendidly in the sunshine of God's love." Neither is it strange that the supreme gift of the beatific vision should be promised to the heart and not to the head. Blessed are the pure in heart, for they shall see God!

It must be that there is something like this in the case of those who, along with the Apostle Paul, find that power is made perfect in weakness. We become sensitive to God! Our very frailty becomes our strength. This poor instrument of ailing flesh and aching nerve which brings us so much pain, and burdens us with a weariness beyond belief, becomes by the grace of God a sure medium for the reception of God. It becomes a true conductor. We are charged with the electric energy of divine possession. When Jesus was here, it seemed as though the weak, the sick, the pain-stricken, suffering men and women and children were the objects of His peculiar care. It seemed as though they had a special claim upon Him and as though He admitted the claim. It seemed, too, as though they in some special way were sympathetic with Him—keyed, so to speak, to His mood and His spirit. And it seems as though the analogy would hold good in the life which you and I have to live. They that are whole need not a physician; and we pervert and abuse that law, and in robust health and in the rush of life with its thrill and passion we are prone to leave God out of account. But in the days or years of weakness and suffering, then we find Him again or He finds us, and we feel ourselves in a special way the object of His love and care. So possessed of God, or so possessing Him, we triumph over our frail mortality. Stonings and scourgings, shipwreck and robber malice, frost and fever, and all the pangs of persecution and all the agonies of the stake in the flesh—what are they to this heroic Paul? And weak men and women amongst ourselves, the nerves raw with suffering, always ailing, aching, weary, the days full of pain, the nights heavy with the sleepless hours—these men and women in the home, in the office, in the schoolroom, in the pulpit, in the sickroom, on land and sea, over every continent and island, work righteousness, subdue kingdoms, quench the violence of fire, stop the mouths of lions, turn aside the edge of the sword—find that power is made perfect in weakness. God be praised for the heroic sufferer! The world would be a sad place without the like of you!

Wherefore, "comfort ye, comfort ye, My people, and speak ye comfortably to Jerusalem, saith your God!" Yes; but do you know the meaning of the word you use? What is comfort? Something soothing, inducing a placid, sweet content, an anodyne for the soul? Indeed, but it is nothing of the kind. Com-fort—the root is "fortis," strength. We get it in fortitude, and fortify, and fort, and fortress. This is the comfort our God shall give you. The Holy Spirit shall be to you a Comforter—shall fortify your soul, though heart and flesh fail, shall make your mind a fortress impregnable and secure. You shall not despair. Pain is always painful and weakness is hard to bear. But take courage and endure; take heart of hope, aspire; such days as yours are filled with blessing for mankind. One-half of your life has been taken from you at a stroke? Yes, but the half that remains is greater than the whole. Jesus died on Calvary. The world's hope is a Cross. After Golgotha, the open Grave. You shall gloriously preach the glorious Gospel of the blissful God in your suffering and pain. We are not ashamed of the Gospel, because it is Power. And Power is made perfect in weakness.

# THE BOMBARDMENTS OF GOD

Dr. Stidger is not simply an engaging personality; he is a startling phenomenon. No man among us has come nearer mastering the art of preaching to the moving-picture-jazz-mind in a world on wheels, which asks for a method of approach of which our fathers never so much as dreamed. As much a journalist as a preacher, he knows the cinematographic quality of the popular mind, to reach which he uses a Gospel spotlight. It was not enough to recast the service, he has actually invented a new kind of Symphonic Sermon. If his methods are always picturesque, and at times astounding, they are but the devices whereby an alert, human-hearted preacher seeks to reach and win the hurrying crowds to the service of his Master: the results of which he reports in *Standing Room Only*.

A West Virginian now in his fortieth year, Dr. Stidger was educated at Allegheny College, Brown University, and the Divinity School of Boston University, and was ordained to the Methodist ministry in 1914. His first charge was Calvary Church, San Francisco, 1913-16; then the First Church of San José, serving the while as a truck driver in France during the Great War. In 1920 he went to St. Mark's Church, Detroit, finding a huge building, empty and bare, which he transformed into a busy, crowded church known all over the land; which he has just left to take up a new work in the Linwood Boulevard Church of Kansas City.

Meantime, he has written at least twenty books of many sorts, ranging from *Soldier Silhouettes* and *Star Dust from the Dugouts* to *Adventures in Humanity*, a study of *Henry Ford*, *Flash Lights of Seven Seas*, *The Symphonic Sermon*, and *A Book of Sunsets*.

# THE BOMBARDMENTS OF GOD

WILLIAM L. STIDGER, D.D.

LINWOOD BOULEVARD METHODIST CHURCH, KANSAS CITY

*And suddenly a light from Heaven flashed round him; he dropped to the ground.* Acts 9: 3 (Moffatt Translation).

There was power in that light! It knocked Saul down. Light always has power in it. There is the scientific intimation that some of these days, when the coal plays out and the oil and gas have been used up, and we shall need more power than tumbling waterfalls and rushing streams can furnish, we shall learn to harness the power that is concealed in the light-rays of the bombarding sun.

The other day I was in the General Electric experimental laboratories. A young preacher who had worked there for eight years took me through the plant. First we went through the great machine shops where they were building gigantic generators, that had to be lifted by colossal electrical cranes which were marked "One Hundred Tons," meaning that these cranes would lift such a load. After we had spent the morning watching the building and testing of these huge generators—the largest in the world, the kind they use at Niagara Falls—my friend said: "Now, I will take you into the laboratories where they are dealing with real power."

We came to a little room, the outside of which was darkened, indicating that an experiment was being carried on which needed darkness. Being a privileged character, my friend pushed the door open cautiously, and we edged our way in. The room was occupied by a little man with glasses. I was later informed that he was one of the expert experimental scientists of the world.

"Well, what are you doing now?" my friend asked the scientist.

"Stand by and I'll show you," answered the experimenter.

We stood by and watched one of the miracles of tomorrow coming to pass. It was in this very room that tungsten was discovered as a metal, and some of the most remarkable discoveries of radio have been developed, including a loud speaker that will revolutionize the whole radio business. It is because of this that I say that we saw the working out of one of the miracles of tomorrow.

There was a simple machine, so constructed that it could throw a bombardment of electrons from an electrical arc. These electrons were thrown for a distance of five feet through a piece of glass. I was permitted to watch this experiment through a lead glass shade. It would have been dangerous to watch it any other way. It was easy to see the path of the electrons. They made a path like a shooting star falling through our atmosphere. I asked the scientist if those were the electrons that we saw in that luminous path of light. He replied, "The thing you see is not the bombardment of electrons, but the effect of these electrons as they pass through the air."

The experimenter then put some germs and spores of bacteria in the path of the bombarding electrons. The electrons killed the germs instantly. Then he put pieces of crystal in the path of the electrons. Within a few seconds he turned off the bombardment of electrons, and picked up the crystals. They were glowing with a brilliant luminosity, and yet there was not a single bit of heat. The electrons had done something to the electrons of the crystals. They had been changed in a miraculous way. That piece of crystal, the scientist told us, would continue to glow that way for two hours and a half.

"What has happened to it we do not know as yet," he said; "that is what we are trying to discover. We think that we are on the trail of a revolutionary discovery; something that may reveal untold power."

I felt as if I stood on the brink of some further discovery of one of those innumerable secrets that God keeps for man until he has enough ingenuity to seek for it and find it. Then I remembered a scene in the New Testament, a man named Saul who was a killer. One day he walked along a certain highway, and suddenly upon his soul there came a terrific bombardment of light from heaven. His soul was in the direct pathway of that light. For a few seconds that bombardment of spiritual electrons was so powerful that it knocked him down, and blinded his eyes. But something happened to Saul in that bombardment of power from on high; something happened that did the same three things that happened in the experiment that I watched in the laboratories.

First, the bombardment of light and power from on high killed the sin in Saul! It killed the hate, the anger, the prejudice, the cruelty. The second thing which the bombardment of light and power did to Saul was to make him glow with a new light in his own soul. He was luminous with Christ from that moment on. That is what always happens to a soul when it gets into the path of the bombardment of the light and power of God. He was no longer Saul. He was now Paul. He was no longer an enemy of God. He was God's Advocate. He was no longer a killer. He was a Lover. His soul glowed with light. His face shone from within with a strange beauty.

Herndon used to say of Lincoln: "He was odd-looking, but when that gray eye and that face and those features were lit up by the inward soul in fires of emotion, then it was that all the apparently ugly features sprang into organs of beauty, or disappeared in the sea of inspiration that flooded his face. Sometimes it appeared as if Lincoln was fresh from the hands of his Creator."

The third proof that Saul had put himself in the pathway of the bombarding light was that something had happened to him. He didn't know just what it was, but he knew that something had happened. He knew it because he was different. He had a different viewpoint. He loved people. He could not explain what had happened to the spiritual electrons of his soul, any more than the scientist can explain what had happened to the electrons of that crystal in the laboratory; but he knew that something had happened. And it was something so beautiful, so revolutionary, that it changed his body, his mind, and his name.

Now there are always a lot of foolish people around who have to have everything explained or they will not believe. But I noticed that the scientist was working on Faith throughout his experiment. He did not understand what was happening. He admitted it to us when I questioned him. He was simply feeling his way carefully, by Faith. In truth that is the way most great scientific discoveries come about. The trained mind reaches out by Faith, feeling dimly but confidently through the night, through the mist of uncertainty, "thinking the thoughts of God after Him," with reverence, and love and wistfulness, until suddenly the path is lighted ahead, and he sees, knows, and understands; and a great scientific formula is discovered.

Every great experiment is an adventure in Faith.

It is often a daring adventure. It is always a glorious adventure. There in the laboratory, that young scientist—modest, unassuming, with an old blouse on—was playing with lightning, shooting electrons, bombarding the air, reaching out into the unknown, into Eternity, into God's secrets, seeking, seeking for some new thing to help mankind. Thank God for the Faith of the scientists!

There are several ways in which we may put ourselves in the pathway of God's spiritual bombardments. First, by getting into the mood of worship. It is a sort of spiritual setting-up exercise. We have to get our souls ready for worship if we expect to worship truly. Stained-glass windows, pipe organs, subdued lights, hymns, ritual, all get us into the mood. I know not, and no other man knows of any better way to get into the mood of worship than to go to church. No man can expect to receive the bombardment of God's spiritual electrons of power and light and have his life transformed, unless he is willing to put himself in the pathway of that bombardment by getting in the mood of worship. A religious service will evoke the mood of worship. A symphony will produce the same mood, as will a sunset, a dawn, a thunderstorm, a violet bed in a mossy crevice, a tangle of arbutus, a burst of love, a great anthem, a Sistine Madonna, a Transfiguration, a white "David" rising in the power of beauty, youth, and love; a "Moses," regnant with power.

Second, we must get into the spirit of prayer if we expect to receive this bombardment of light and power. Church prayer is so often a blatant, mechanical, hard thing. The preacher suddenly launches into a prayer because it is in the order of service, or because he feels it must be gone through with. We have established a simple thing in our church to suggest the mood of prayer in our souls. We have erected a lighted cross above the altar. At prayer-time a prayer-hymn is sung, the first verse in full voice, the second verse softly, and then we hum the third verse, while the choir softly sings the words. Then, gradually, like twilight falling, the lights go off and the cross is illuminated. The people sit in the light of that cross, with the echo of the prayer-hymn in their souls, touched, subdued, bowed in a mood of prayer. Then comes the Prayer, and following the "Amen" a softly chanted prayer while the people are still bowed.

Out in California at the Exposition they built a Fine Arts Palace. Then the architect built a beautiful colonnade in a crescent shape around the Arts Palace. This colonnade was hung with flowers, planted with shrubbery, and lined with beautiful statuary. I remember that Piccirilli's "The Outcast" was there, and a hundred other pieces. There was a lagoon outside of the crescent colonnade. One dreamed of Athens, Rome, Italy, Art, Music, Poetry, as one drifted through the colonnade. It was necessary to go through the colonnade before getting to the pictures.

The architect told me that he built the approach to the Fine Arts Palace in this fashion because most of those who visited the Exhibition would come from the Zone, the Palace of Machinery or Horticulture, the blatant cries of popcorn venders, the rattle of wheels, and the shout of fakers; and they would be in no mood to feel, much less to appreciate pictures. Therefore he made it necessary for them to pass through this mood-making colonnade before they got to the pictures. Then they were in the mood of feeling and understanding great art. So it is with prayer.

One must have the right surroundings and atmosphere if one expects to change the electrons of the soul. This does not conflict with the first qualification that I have mentioned: that of mood. Mood is internal; atmosphere is external. One must have the right atmosphere to develop certain qualities. Emerson speaks it thus: "Men are what their mothers make them. You may as well ask a loom which weaves Huckaback why it does not make cashmere; expect poetry from an engineer, or a chemical discovery from a jobber."

In this same laboratory was developed the metal that we call tungsten. Or, rather, it was discovered, for it is a metal all by itself. It was always in existence, but we have only recently found it. It was made possible only because of what scientists call a Hydrogen Furnace. Only in the atmosphere of a hydrogen furnace was it possible to experiment with tungsten, to which we owe the tungsten lamp, and the X-ray. It is wonderful to watch a hydrogen furnace burning, with its slow, flickering, greenish light, not so intensely hot, but of a certain atmosphere. In that atmosphere alone is it possible to develop and work with tungsten.

So certain surroundings, certain atmospheres are conducive to spiritual power. Under certain conditions power may be transmitted. In a certain atmosphere one is liable to spiritual revelations. Great men have always retired into solitude for their revelations, their meditations, their moments of deep insight into spiritual things. Jesus retired to the mountain-sides; John the Baptist to the wilderness; John of Patmos to a lonely island. Thus a child raised in the atmosphere of a good home, of a Christian church, of high thoughts and true, will be much more likely to get in the pathway of the great bombardment.

There is an atmosphere about certain men that makes all who meet them taller, better, happier! Julia Ward Howe's husband is said to have carried about with him the "Air of Freedom." Dan Crawford said that "Stanley knew there was a Christ because there was a Livingstone." He felt the truth of a living Christ because he stood in the atmosphere of the life of that great soul. We need the atmosphere of a happy home, of the church, of Christian friends, of quiet places for meditation, if we expect to catch the bombardment of the light and power of God that will illuminate and transform and beautify our souls. Some find just the right atmosphere they want in a garden:

I never knew Thee, Lord, until
  My garden brought us face to face,
Revealed Thy gracious miracle
  Of sun and seed in little space.

Since I have seen Thy alchemy
  Change the earth-brown bulbs to living gold
Of daffodils, Eternity
  Has seemed a simple truth to hold.

The incense-breath of mignonette
  Has summoned me to vespers too,
And may I nevermore forget
  To lift my heart, as pansies do!

No dim cathedral is as still
  As twilight in this holy place;
I never knew Thee, Lord, until
  My garden brought us face to face.

So sings Molly Anderson Haley. Her soul needs the atmosphere of a garden to find God—and not only she but another who sings:

The kiss of the sun for pardon,
  The song of the birds for mirth;
One is nearer God's heart in a garden
  Than anywhere else on earth.

What is the atmosphere that you need to get nearer to God? I know not what it is. But you do. That is God's secret with you. He has made a rendezvous with your soul for that Divine meeting. He has given you and none other to know. Yours is the glory of that knowledge. It is like a lovers' tryst; only you and God to know where it is. To some it may be a garden; to some a mountain-top; to some "beside the still waters"; to some a starlit night; to some a home atmosphere; to some the dim aisles of a cathedral; to some the haunts of boyhood. Whatever it is, whatever atmosphere you need, find it out as carefully as you learn what foods suit you best, what colors suit you in your clothing, what perfumes, what flowers, and what friends. Live in that atmosphere; find God; and get into the glowing path of His bombardment of spiritual light and power.

Let God bombard you with His light and love! Let Him bombard you as once I saw Him bombard the snow-white beauty of Mont Blanc with His morning sunlight. Let Him bombard your soul as He bombards the earth with the storm; as He bombards the meadows in springtime with flowers, and blossoms, and wistful wings; as He bombards the forest with color at autumn time. Let Him bombard your soul with music as He bombards the Æolian harp with His blustering winds to make immortal music; as He bombards the heart of a poet.

There was once an upper room where men met for the purpose of worship. There, in the sweet mood of reverence, they talked about immortality and Christ, and of their love for each other, and for Him. In their loneliness their hearts were deeply stirred with love for each other. And, because they had put themselves in the mood of worship, in the mood of prayer, the quiet chamber of silence became a spiritual sanctuary before they were aware of it, because they had gotten into the burning atmosphere of fraternal love. Suddenly the room was illuminated with a strange light, and a sound of a mighty rushing wind, and their hearts were deeply stirred; and the Holy Spirit of Social Passion and Brotherhood was born in their souls. Before they knew it they were caught in the burning, blinding, awakening pathway of a celestial bombardment of power and light from God.

The same thing had happened to a group as had happened to one Saul, who became Paul. When it was all over, the sin was killed in their souls as it was in Paul's, and their lives were illuminated with a strange white light. Something had happened, and the Church of Jesus was born on earth. These strangely beautiful things always happen when man gets into the burning pathway of light and power from the heart of God:

Oh, glory of the lighted mind;
How dull I'd been, how dead, how blind;
The station brook to my new eyes
Was babbling out of Paradise.

Oh, glory of the lighted soul;
The dawn comes up on Bradlow knoll,
The dawn with glittering on the grasses;
The dawn which pass and never passes!

# HOW ONE MAN DISCOVERED GOD

An Iowan, born in 1876, educated at Dixon College and Rider Divinity School, Dr. Adams was ordained to the Universalist ministry in 1905. He held pastorates at Indianapolis, at Spokane, Washington, at Urbana and Elgin, Illinois, until 1923, when he came to the pulpit of the Church of Our Father, Detroit. During the World War he served as First Lieutenant in the infantry, and as instructor in Camp Grant and Camp Lee; and after the War was the first State Chaplain of the American Legion in Illinois.

Besides a number of brochures dealing with moral and spiritual issues growing out of the Great War, Dr. Adams has given us two very striking books, the first being an analysis of the principles of Jesus in the Sermon on the Mount, arranged for group study, entitled *Did Jesus Mean It?*—one of the most searching little books I have ever seen. His latest book, *Rediscovered Countries,* has to do with the basic ideas of Christian faith in the light of modern life and thought, a valuable book to put into the hands of young folk who are perplexed in their religious thinking.

How the prophet Hosea turned a desolating tragedy into a deeper revelation—finding God anew where so many lose Him and become cynical—is here expounded with clarity of style and persuasive power, showing us how to meet those things in life which are far worse than death by the transfiguring grace of spiritual vision.

## HOW ONE MAN DISCOVERED GOD

FRANK DURWARD ADAMS, D.D.

CHURCH OF OUR FATHER, DETROIT

*How can I give thee up, Ephraim? How shall I cast thee off, Israel? . . . My heart is turned within me, my compassions are kindled together. I will not execute the fierceness of mine anger, I will not return to destroy Ephraim. For I am God, and not man; the Holy One in the midst of thee; and I will not come in wrath.* Hosea 11: 8-9.

The story of Hosea turns upon a tragedy, such a tragedy as has wrecked thousands of lives. In his young manhood he fell in love with Gomer, the daughter of Diblaim, and in due course they were married. Three children were born to them, two sons and a daughter. In the meantime the nation of Israel was passing through critical days; and the names Hosea gave to his children are symbolical of what he believed God's attitude to be towards his backsliding people.

There is no hint that Hosea ever doubted his wife's fidelity. But one day he lost her! Not by death. That would have been bearable, perhaps even a means of spiritual blessing and understanding. He lost her because she was unfaithful to him, unfaithful to her marriage vows, unfaithful to the little children whom she had brought into the world. Gomer became a wanton—the worst fate that can befall any woman. Only imperfectly can we realize what that means; for it is only through actual experience that we ever fully understand anything. But we can imagine something of Hosea's emotions, something of his heart agony, bitterness, and black despair. And I think we might have excused him if he had gone to pieces, if he had become hard and bitter and cynical; even if he himself had plunged into the same social undercurrent into which he had seen the wife of his young manhood disappear.

But Hosea didn't do that. He did an amazing thing, an almost incredible thing. He took his wife back to his home and his heart. Nay, more. He went out and sought and rescued her from the shame into which she had fallen. Their home was reëstablished, and the white flame glowed once more upon the altar of their mutual love.

But a great new Something was coming to birth in Hosea's heart. A wonderful Something it must have been, for men do not commonly act in this way. He was beginning to understand a lot of things. He had probably tried to put the remembrance of his erring wife quite out of his mind. But he could not do it. He had doubtless tried to nurse the memory of his wrongs, tried to make that memory grow and grow into a cankering bitterness in his heart. But he could not do it. Perhaps he had tried to transmute the holy love of a third of a lifetime into an unforgiving hate. But he could not do it. He discovered with amazement that his heart was too big, his spirit too magnanimous, his love too invincible. Somehow he understood our human frailty too well to do that. So he just flung wide his door, his arms, and his heart, and the penitent crept broken-hearted back to their sheltering embrace.

And a great new Something was coming to birth in this man's reason also. His brain was as clear and his logic as keen as his heart was great. Hosea was a prophet by instinct and a theologian by nature. He lived in a day when men were just beginning to grope their way slowly, painfully, out of the smaller and cruder thought of God of the primitive Hebrews. Dimly but yet surely they were coming to think of Jehovah as a Being just a little more intimate and dear than the mere judge and ruler of a tribe. And when Hosea was agonizing under the cloud which had fallen upon his own life, like a flash of sunlight a great truth burst before his eyes. Something said to him: "Hosea, Hosea, is not your God at least as great in his love and compassion as you are? What your finite love has impelled you to do for your erring, repentant wife, think you not God in his infinite love will do for his erring, repentant children? Though you are but a man, whose frame is dust, your love has triumphed over all less worthy emotions. Must not the love of God be greater yet than yours?"

The thought was compelling, sublime. And as it pierced his heart, arrow-tipped with a truth he could not gainsay, his horizons were pushed out, his heaven was lifted up, and in that moment of unearthly vision Hosea's God became the tenderly divine-human, human-divine husband, father, and protector of his people. Israel had played the part of an erring spouse, a bride gone into wantonness. How well Hosea understood the meaning of that! Yet he had taken his wife back to his arms. And, lo! God was Hosea multiplied by infinity, yearning over Israel, loving Israel with an everlasting love, and calling Israel back to his embrace. And out of that revelation, came gushing as it were a virgin spring out of the midst of the blackest waters that can overwhelm any human soul, methinks Hosea must have read the words I have taken as a text: "How can I give thee up, Ephraim? How shall I cast thee off, Israel? . . . My heart is turned within me, my compassions are kindled together. I will not execute the fierceness of mine anger, I will not return to destroy Ephraim. For I am God, and not man; the Holy One in the midst of thee; and I will not come in wrath." And thenceforth this becomes the keynote of Hosea's message.

Now it will be profitable to note the several steps by which Hosea came to this point of spiritual understanding. Experience is something shared by all of us. It differs in detail with each individual; yet it is surprising how very like human experience is on the whole. It is calculated to open the door to wisdom: yet how few enter into wisdom thereby! It is a common proverb that experience is a dear teacher. True, but we usually reject her lessons. Yet this suggests the reason why Hosea learned something in those agonizing days which multitudes of others do not learn. His experience was not unique. Hosts of others have had to face the same ordeal, or others quite as trying. But Hosea emerged a different man. And what is the secret of that difference? Simply *the spirit* in which he met his trial and dealt with it. And I discover three distinct steps in the prophet's spiritual evolution. If we note each of them carefully, it will become perfectly clear why Hosea came forth a conqueror out of circumstances in the midst of which most men crumple and surrender.

First of all, *he had to meet a crisis.* He had to face a certain, definite situation. It is not my present purpose to go into any discussion of the why and wherefore of such bitter experiences. That in itself would suffice for many sermons. Let me only remark that they seem to be indispensable. Sometimes a quick, sharp, stinging blow is necessary to wake us up. There are times when we need a shock. It is quite possible for our circumstances to be too easy. Perhaps the world needed the shock of that awful war to open our eyes to the huge gulf that yawns between our theories of human brotherhood and our practice of the same. At any rate, one day Hosea came biff! against just such a blow. Had he been suspicious before? Probably not. His love was blind; as love should always be except to the good. But when the terrible truth was no longer to be denied!—well, it is better perhaps to leave the rest to the imagination. Note only this momentous fact: Hosea was facing an awful crisis.

But, as I have said, others have had to meet just such crises. Some have had to face this identical situation. One very close to me stood one tragic day, with his four little children about him, crushed with the knowledge that his wife was gone, just as Gomer had gone, away with another. But these things have to be met when they come. Our loved ones go astray and break our hearts. Our business fails and we face financial ruin. We fail professionally, and great ideals and ambitions crumble. Death puts out his cold finger and stills the heart upon which we have builded the hopes of a lifetime. It is a crisis and we have to meet it. Just as Hosea met the soul-paralyzing truth that he had lost into worse than death the wife of his young manhood.

But there was something else Hosea had to do. He not only had to face the crisis. *He had to deal with it.* This is the second step in his progress. He had to do something; something more than to wring his hands and weep and bewail his lot. It was up to him! His home was desolate; his little children were motherless; his neighbors were inquisitive and supercilious; his own heart was aching with a void that could not be filled. You must do something, Hosea. What will it be? You are standing now at the parting of the ways. What you do now will mean much. It will determine the fate of five priceless souls—your own, your wife's, and the souls of three innocent little children. What are you going to do, Hosea, what are you going to do?

What would you do if you were in his place? What *do* you do in the face of any crisis? Do you crumple and fall down before it like a man of straw; or do you stand up and defy and master it? I suppose we shall never settle the world-old question as to whether the environment controls the individual or the individual the environment. The truth probably lies somewhere between the two, as it usually lies midway between any two extremes. But it is interesting to note what Hosea evidently believed about that. He might have given up. He might have concluded that the circumstances were too much for him. He might have argued that environment is the determining factor in human life, anyhow; and how could he be expected to stand up against such a combination of evil circumstances? He was a mere pawn on a chessboard! Let Fate push him whither it would!

Be it far from me to minimize the influence of environment upon human life and character. I know it has influence. If I did not so believe I would not be striving with might and main to help change our social environment. But here is a fact to consider. What a man *does* in the presence of his environment, in the face of any combination of circumstances, is of a great deal more importance than the circumstances themselves. He can master it, or be mastered by it. And the only explanation of great lives is that they have chosen to be masters.

What did Hosea do? Did he yield? Did he follow the line of least resistance? The neighbors said, "Divorce your wife; put her away; your self-respect demands it." His own pride said, "I have been sorely wronged; I must justify myself and my children." Mrs. Grundy said, "You bring yourself right down on her moral level if you tolerate her another minute." All that was the voice of environment, of social conformity, the voice to which we nearly always hearken. But did Hosea hearken to it? Indeed he did not! He proved that, in the hands of a real man, environment is a puppet, circumstances a rope of sand. He ignored his smirking neighbors; he stifled the voice of his own false pride; he defied Mrs. Grundy—and went out after the one who was lost! That is Hosea's answer to the world-old question of the power of human environment. Take it for what you may think it is worth.

When one you love goes astray, what do you do? When your business goes to smash, when high hopes fail, when death's icy finger touches a heart you adore and stops its beating, what do you do? You have to do something, even as Hosea did. Your future is shaped by what you do then. So was Hosea's. Listen to this bit of a story.

> There was a little American missionary who was going home to stay after twenty years of service. At the request of the Board she stopped off at the Leper Colony, in the Pacific, in order to make a report. Soon after she reached home, she discovered a small white spot on her hand; and on consulting a physician, found it was leprosy. Without breathing a word of it to any one, she bade her family and friends a cheerful good-by, and came straight back to that Leper Colony, where she took up her work among the outcasts. Never an outcry, never a groan, not even a plea for sympathy.

Can you imagine what must have passed between that woman's soul and God in the hour which marked that decision? She had to do something. And to see what was going on in her heart would be to behold another Gethsemane—and the glory that came after it.

But there remained a third step to be taken. Hosea had to face the crisis, indeed; likewise, he had to deal with it; and then he had to determine *what effect it was to have upon himself.* This last was the only one of the three steps which was altogether in his control. Perhaps he was not largely responsible for the conditions he was obliged to face. However he might have elected to deal with the situation, he might not have succeeded in winning the erring one back. But at this point he held the absolute mastery. He, and he alone, had the power to say what effect this experience was to have upon himself, and in what spirit he was to meet it and carry it through, and whether it was to leave him an embittered cynic or teach him the greatest of the lessons of life. This was wholly in Hosea's hands, a deliberate moral choice.

The decision turned upon whether he was ready to learn life's greatest lesson. He was ready. And his Teacher was ready. Oh, the unwearied patience of God! Not patience alone, but wise and loving timeliness. The Spirit of God breaks through no doors, picks no locks, forces no entrances. He enters only when we are ready, and then he comes in such a wonderful way! In the Gita, one of the great scriptures of India, we find these words: "When the pupil is ready the Master appeareth. When most thou needest knowledge, the next link in thy chain, wait in patience and confidence; for, lo! suddenly at thy hand shalt come what thou neededst." How like the words of our own greater Scripture, where the Spirit saith:

"Behold, I stand at the door and knock. If any man hear my voice, and open the door, I will come in to him, and will sup with him, and he with me."

Hosea opened his heart for the lesson. It was severe at the moment; but his part was just to open the door. Such a combination of circumstances had the power to make him a snarler or a prophet, a cynic or a saint. He chose to be a prophet and a saint, and it was a deliberate choice. And Hosea stands as a type of a universal truth. The law works identically with all. When your business goes crashing, when your professional hopes go glimmering, when a high ambition fails, when the footsteps of Death come stealing noiselessly across your threshold, one thing, and only one, is in your absolute control. You cannot change what has gone before. You might have changed it once, but you cannot now. The past is dead, and you can only bury it. Neither can you control in any great measure the effect which your manner of dealing with the situation may have upon the other persons involved in it. That is all taken out of your hands. But you *can* say what the effect of all this is to be upon yourself; you *can* elect in what spirit you will meet and deal with it; you *can* determine what sort of a man or woman it is going to make of you in the days to come. At such moments the invincible spirit of Henley's "Invictus" may stand us in noble stead:

Out of the night that covers me,
 Black as the pit from pole to pole,
I thank whatever gods may be,
 For my unconquerable soul.

In the fell clutch of circumstance
 I have not winced nor cried aloud.
Under the bludgeonings of chance
 My head is bloody but unbowed.

. . . . .

It matters not how strait the gate,
 How charged with punishments the scroll,
I am the master of my fate:
 I am the captain of my soul!

Hosea recognized the hand of God. Now I do not say that Divine Wisdom deliberately brought all these things to pass. But Hosea needed a shock to open his mind to an eternal truth. Otherwise he might have gone on to the end of the chapter, just a common, good enough fellow, but never a great prophet of God. Man's extremity is God's opportunity; and this was God's opportunity. We do not choose suffering and ill fortune for our children; but when they come we know how to turn them to their advantage. So the mind of Hosea opened just at the moment when God and the circumstances came together to turn the scale of human history. The man, the circumstances, and God met in one of those vital combinations which have always resolved the crises of human life. And Hosea, born into the spirit of prophecy by a single heart-racking experience, in the vision of one pregnant moment understood that he was acting on a finite scale the part of God in the infinite drama of the world's redemption. As he had done, as he was doing and would do, even so God has done, was doing and would do! Amazing thought, marvelous truth! He had saved one, because she was dear to his heart. God would save all, because all are dear to the heart of the Eternal. God, the infinitely greater, more loving and more compassionate, is dealing in just that way with his erring children.

It seemeth to me that this was the natal day of man's right thought of God. A home was reëstablished, type and symbol of the coming era of good will, of which men have long been dreaming as the millennium, Paradise, the kingdom of heaven. An erring soul had come purified up out of the crucible of pain. Husband, wife, and children were reconciled, symbol of the coming harmony when God's wise and gracious purpose shall be fully achieved.

Now it only remains for us to apply this great truth to ourselves. I would have you know that what was true of Hosea is true also of you. Hosea found God. So can you find him—and in precisely the same way. Find him in your experience, and in your spiritual reaction to that experience. The secret of the prophet's illumination may be summed up in a sentence. He entered into the meaning of elemental human experience. Just common, everyday, human experience. I know we are prone to suppose that we must seek God in some occult, mysterious, supernatural way. No doubt God is sometimes thus found; but as a general rule that is all wrong. That is the stumbling-block which keeps so many from the true wisdom of life. The more occult, the more mysterious, the more supernatural the means is, the less apt you are, in my opinion, to find God at all.

Suppose you begin looking carefully into the experience through which you are right now passing. What of that bereavement that has lately come to you? What of that misfortune, that grievous burden, that hope deferred? What of the ever-present problems and perplexities of your home and business, from which none of us is free? What are they good for, if they do not bring us a little closer to the beating heart of things? What are they good for, if we cannot see in them the working out of some great principle of truth, some purpose of an infinite love? If they do not mean this, they mean nothing, and the universe is chaos.

Thus we see that there is no substitute for experience; no substitute, so far as I can see, for suffering. You will not find a single exception to this. The great souls have all been made perfect through suffering. But only when they were able to see in it the loving heart and hand of God, just as Hosea did. As some one has lately said, "Misfortune opens the soul to illuminations which in prosperity are unseen." Yes, I know such doctrine is not popular in our piping times of prosperity. I know we like to think there is some easy way. But there is no easy way, if by that you mean the getting of understanding without the experience out of which understanding is born. It is impossible in the very nature of things, as it was impossible for Hosea to know God without the experience that broke his heart. Did not Jesus himself have to suffer and die to show us the way to the heart of God? And without that suffering and death Jesus would mean little or nothing to the world today.

"But," some one exclaims, "I cannot believe that we must go stumbling on through all eternity poor, bruised, maimed and suffering souls, in order to understand!" Poor, bruised, maimed, suffering? Ah, that all depends upon what you get out of your experience. If you only feel that it hurts you, that you don't deserve it, that it is without meaning and purpose, just so long your soul will be bruised, maimed, and despairing. And just so long you will stumble in the way. But when you understand that it is *the hurt that heals and reveals,* what a difference! The hurt that makes you wise; the hurt that deepens and broadens your sympathies; the hurt that makes it possible for you to understand the meaning of all the world's suffering; the hurt that even reveals to you the heart of the Infinite in His brooding love and compassion for all His suffering, stumbling, blundering children. The hurt that heals and reveals! Then you stumble no longer, but walk erect in the white light that streams upon your path.

Volumes of philosophy have been written by those who sought to discover the meaning of pain and to fathom the eternal mysteries of God. But with all their learning and labor they have never carried us beyond this simple truth. In your experience you will find God *if you look for him there.* Lay that to your heart. In it is a balm for every wound. Be guided by it, and you will become an agent of God through whose ministry others may come into the same healing wisdom and light.

Yes, Hosea, we understand you now. Your suffering has afforded us a glimpse into the very Heart of the Eternal.

And if the vision come to thee,
  Revealed by inward sign,
Earth will be full of Deity,
  And with His glory shine!

# HAVING OR BEING

A Bostonian by birth, educated at Harvard and at Union Theological Seminary, Dr. Fitch was ordained to the Congregational ministry in 1903, his first pastorate being in Flushing, Long Island. After a fruitful ministry in Mt. Vernon Church, Boston, he became President of Andover Theological Seminary, Cambridge, in 1909, and eight years later Professor of the History of Religion in Amherst College. He resigned with President Meiklejohn, and is now Professor of the History of Religion in Carleton College.

Some of us can never forget the Lyman Beecher Lectures by Dr. Fitch at Yale, in 1919-20, entitled *Preaching and Paganism,* in which he examined, as with an X-ray, the influences and tendencies making for the dechristianization of modern life. The erect figure, the soft, exquisitely modulated voice, the ripe fruits of a rich culture, the limpid, vivid, flexible style, the sparkling insight, the scintillating satire, and at times the mood of mingled joy and pathos, as old as the world and as mysterious as the voices behind the winds, in which our hearts were strangely warmed and spiritual realities became incandescent—it lingers in memory like a vision; and we knew why he is one of the most fascinating and challenging preachers of his generation.

No wonder we read everything he has written, from *The Religion of an Undergraduate* to his stinging little essay in study of the Church and the Changing Order, including his extraordinary college story, *None So Blind,* which deserved a wider vogue than it enjoyed. Yet, somehow, more than anything else one would prefer to have a little book of his prayers, in which he is at once a surgeon, a physician, and a God-anointed priest and prophet of the soul.

# HAVING OR BEING

ALBERT PARKER FITCH

CARLETON COLLEGE, NORTHFIELD, MINN.

*For what shall it profit a man if he gain the whole world and lose his own soul?* Matthew 16: 26.

These are rather distasteful words; and it might be well for us, first, to examine into the causes of our half-instinctive reaction against them. Nearly all human prejudices are the product of human ignorance; if we understand the sayings of Jesus it may be that we shall not dislike them. The first cause of our irritation with the words is due, I fancy, to the striking and epigrammatic manner in which Jesus contrasts the "world" and the "soul," as though he would indicate that there was an absolute cleavage between material and spiritual things, that each was hostile to and mutually exclusive of the other. Hence we feel something of the ascetic spirit here, a repressive or negative attitude toward life.

But such feelings are wholly unjustified by the facts. There never was a being less ascetic in temper than Jesus. He ate with publicans and sinners. His scandalized contemporaries called him gluttonous and a winebibber. He offered the sharpest possible contrast to the really ascetic John the Baptist in his interest in and participation in all joyous, normal, human activity. Nor was there anything negative in his attitude toward life. He looked out and not in, was aggressive, optimistic, positive in person and teaching. His whole conception of his mission was not that of the exposing and ejecting of error, but of the discovery and cultivation of that truth which, by its very presence, leaves no place for error.

"I came," he said, "not to destroy, but to fulfill." His consistent method in dealing with human lives was to save them through development rather than repression; he interpreted men's instincts, sometimes disciplined them, but never repressed them. He did not stand behind and drive, but he said, "I go before them and my sheep *follow* me because they know my voice."

This positive, liberating attitude is nowhere more beautifully illustrated than in his calling of his first disciples, Peter and James and John. They were peasant fishermen, and Jesus found them one morning on the Sea of Galilee engaged in their perilous and fascinating task. Did he say to them: Come away from this menial occupation, these humble associations; rid yourselves of all interest in this primitive and unskilled occupation and I will make over your natures into a different and a better life? By no means! What he said was: How glorious a thing it is to be a fisherman! Yours is one of the fundamental and romantic occupations of the world. But a man who has the fisherman's heart deserves a far greater and more valuable chance to express that instinct than you have here. "Come after me and I will make you fishers of men!" Jesus always dealt this way with human life. He so believed in it that he thought that what it chiefly needed was to be given intelligent understanding of itself and then perfect freedom for the higher self-development. No; whatever else is in this text, there is nothing ascetic or negative or repressive here!

But the second reason why we don't like the text is that it seems to us arbitrary, as if Jesus, without giving any reasons for it, were sounding a warning from without about human lives which men must not question but accept. When the modern man is told to do something he wants to know why! The cryptic form into which Jesus' sayings are cast, that oracular air which they possess and which was merely the fashion of his time and country, partly account for this unpleasant impression. The fact that his sayings have come down to us through the medium of an ecclesiastical organization, and that we associate them with the conventional authority of preacher and Church, has more to do with it. We distrust ecclesiastical authority because it happens to offer one of the most picturesque forms, and one most often exploited, of arbitrary domination of the wills and consciences of men. And, so often have these words been commended to us on external grounds, that now we think there is no other authority but that behind them. Just as some men have come to distrust, in our day, the political idealism of a democratic government because it has become so associated and confounded with certain debased political and industrial institutions.

But here again we do Jesus a grave injustice. As a matter of fact, one of the most striking things about him was the utter absence in him of any appeal to the external and the artificial. This is what his contemporaries meant when they said: "This man speaks as one having authority and not as the Scribes." What they meant was that other teachers and leaders of their day rested back their doctrine on the Temple ritual, or the customs of the Synagogue or the sayings in the Law and the Prophets, or the Talmud, or the commentaries of the Scribes, but that he spoke out of the fullness of personal experience and gave no other reason for asking assent to his sayings except that of their inherent reasonableness. All his famous words are interpretations of human experience, not impositions upon it. He never made up moral and spiritual laws; he only discovered them. Unless a thing were eternally so Jesus would be the last person in the world to expect you to believe it!

But a third and final reason why we dislike this saying of our Lord is because it does run counter to the dominant interests and the dominant faith of our own generation. We belong to an acquisitive Society; the text does sound a warning against acquisitiveness. We place great emphasis upon the economic basis of life; the means of life appear to us absolutely essential for grasping and enjoying the meaning of life. And, as a general statement, this seems to Jesus rather pathetic and misguided, and even silly. No wonder we dislike the text; it denies our most complacent assumptions and it rebukes some of our most cherished ambitions.

Nevertheless, Jesus was a singularly free and positive spirit, catholic in mind, inclusive in outlook. His only authority was that which comes from the power to see into the heart of things; the force of his teaching resides only in the substance of its doctrine; it is at least worth while to examine what it is that he is saying to us here.

So we come to ask ourselves the meaning of the text. What is Jesus talking about? He is pointing out how important it is that men should maintain a just scale of values. "The end of all education," Lessing once said, "is to make men see things that are big, as big, and things that are small, as small." That is the end of all successful living also. Now, says Jesus, a certain amount of possessions is obviously essential. Men must have food to eat and clothes to wear and a roof to shelter them. They must have these things as the preliminary conditions for the higher and more precious self-expressions.

Material values, then, are real but they have a sort of secondary reality. Spiritual values, the things of the imagination and of the mind, the quick sense of beauty, goodness, truth, these are the ends of life. A basis of material goods is the means towards such ends. But, says Jesus, many men make the means an end in themselves. Thus they create a false scale of values and make small things big, and big things small.

In short, he says, there comes a time in every human life when a man must decide whether he thinks it is more valuable to have or more valuable to be. When that time comes, look out, for if what you have is more than what you are you can neither really own it nor appreciate it, and your possessions, instead of expressing your personality, will obscure, and perhaps destroy, it. Now that's a self-evident truth. Mark Hopkins, the famous president of Williams College, is said to have once given it this picturesque illustration. "How many of you," he said to his senior class, "would accept from me a million dollars at the price of your hearing? Probably a good many of you. How many of you would be willing to be both deaf and dumb for the sake of a million dollars? Perhaps there are some here who would be willing. But if I said to you, how many of you here, for the sake of a million dollars, would be willing to sacrifice both sight and speech and hearing, you would pause, for the time would then have come when you would have to decide whether you would rather have something or be somebody!"

A great and revered teacher quotes from Ruskin the tale of a man who was shipwrecked. Before leaving the sinking vessel he bound about his person a belt containing two hundred sovereigns in gold pieces. Then he adjusted his life preserver before being thrown into the water. But, unhappily, the weight of the gold more than offset the buoyancy of the life-belt and so he sank slowly to the bottom, where he miserably perished. "Now," says Ruskin, with sardonic humor, "as he was thus sinking did he have the gold or did the gold have him?" That man kept his world and lost his self, his soul.

Up in the country, where I live in the summer, there is a great hill, Ascutney Mountain, lying in recumbent majesty along the bank of the Connecticut. Among the farmers you will find the men, who, as they naïvely say, "own the mountain." The title to its upland pastures, its timbered spurs is theirs. But the concept "mountain," its esthetic and spiritual values, means nothing to them. What they really own is determined by the limits of the personality of the owner, and all that mountain means to them is a tract of semi-sterile land and acres of inaccessible, unmarketable timber. But along comes an artist who can paint that mountain and make its eternal majesty, its mute and irrefragable strength, a source of joy and inspiration to his fellow human beings, or a poet, who seeing it, can say, "I will lift up my eyes unto the hills from whence cometh my strength." Now who owns the mountain? The farmer? Of course not. The poet and the artist own it because they understand it; they comprehend it because they are greater than it. So you see what happened. What did it profit the farmer to gain the world bigger than his soul? And what does it matter to the man of personality whether he gains the world or not?

Or, take a final illustration, centuries ago, long before the birth of Jesus, there lived a man in Asia Minor whose palace is just now being dug up because on the ruins of it was built a Greek temple which the archeologists are uncovering. This man's name was Crœsus and he was the richest man of his day and generation. That's all you know about him. He was "as rich as Crœsus." Also in those ancient days there lived a man whose name was Leonidas. When the Persian foe came swarming across the Ægean Sea up to the pass of Thermopylæ he and his little band withstood them there: there he made his body a rampart against the hordes who would enslave Sparta. The Persian horsemen came trampling over him; he perished in his youth. But he had truly lived, he had conquered life. Does he not perfectly illustrate the truth of Jesus' saying? Leonidas saved his soul; he did not need the world. Crœsus had the world; but since it was more than he, what did it profit him?

You see, then, what Jesus means. Only personality has supreme worth. You cannot really gain anything unless you also gain the capacity to own and to use it. What you are must be bigger than what you have!

And now, perhaps, this brings us to the point where we can see what is a chief value of ethical and spiritual meditation and of public worship. An hour like this is given us to restore the balance of life, to save the soul from the world, and to see the world with the soul, to set things in perspective so that the large things of life shall look large, and the small things shall look small. This is a very necessary and a very difficult thing to accomplish because our question is not of exclusive but of relative values. The soul must have possessions, both for its development and its expression. It cannot cut the Gordian knot, as the ascetic would do, by dispensing with them altogether. The question is to find out at what point we cease to have the possessions and they begin to have us. Epictetus, the slave, was a great man in the Roman Empire. But perhaps Marcus Aurelius was a greater. Epictetus had only his soul, but what a soul he had! It made him one of the immortals. But fate set Marcus Aurelius a more difficult task. It gave him all the possessions in the world and bade him save his soul in spite of them, and he did. He used them and did not let them use him, and thus he maintained the just scale of values in a far more difficult area of human experience than fate had assigned to Epictetus.

Just here is where the difficult question lies for every soul. Your question is not "either," "or" but "both," "and." And the precise object of worship is to give that detachment from the partial and the present, and that view of the whole and the eternal which shall produce intellectual, moral, spiritual "good judgment." We come here to return the life to its all-inclusive source, to try to see the present in the light of the ending and the beginning so that we shall not, in gaining our portion of the world, lose the only thing that makes it really ours or really valuable—our own free spirit.

And, finally, this is why we love the Lord Jesus and turn in faith and worship towards him. He perfectly accomplished our task and we gauge ourselves by him. Many of us have seen Mount Washington, looking up at it from Intervale, and it has seemed to us a great mountain. Still we could not know until we had seen the highest. But if we go to northern India and look on the snowy summit of Mount Everest as it seems to pierce the sky, then we know what a mountain can really be. And then we know that Washington is little more than a foothill.

Jesus is our Mount Everest in the human and the

spiritual world. Is my life using "the world" or being used by it? Am I getting too much and slowly being less and less of a man? I cannot tell by comparing myself with other men who stand about where I do. But I may turn to Jesus. I may make His Soul, that overcame the world, my test of my Soul. Then I know. So I go to worship the Father, through Him, that I, too, may gain a just scale of values. For what shall it profit me if I gain all my little world and lose myself, my soul?

# A NEW EARTH

Mr. Phillips is the youngest man in this volume, just now in his first pastorate after leaving the Seminary, and he gives promise of unusual power both as preacher and leader. Born in Jamaica, British West Indies, in 1892, he came to America in 1912, graduating from the Doane Academy, Granville, Ohio, in 1916, and from Denison University in 1919. Entering Union Theological Seminary the same year, he was graduated in 1922, at the same time taking his Master of Arts degree in Columbia University—specializing in sociology.

Having made his first attempt at preaching at the age of seventeen, he had a deal of experience as supply for various churches in his academy and college days, and later in addressing many student conferences and Y.M.C.A. groups—revealing extraordinary gifts as a speaker. As soon as he finished his university and seminary training, he became pastor of the First Baptist Church of Mt. Vernon, New York, and has rapidly advanced in power as a preacher and as a leader of Christian faith and service.

In the following sermon a young man looks forward toward a new earth in which righteousness shall reign over all, consecrating commerce, science, and the fellowship of nations; a rule of God which begins in individual integrity and conquers industrial injustice and world chaos, by the power and passion of Christ. Like so many of our younger preachers, he thinks in terms of one humanity and one Christianity, and his message is at once a challenge and a prophecy.

# A NEW EARTH

HAROLD C. PHILLIPS

FIRST BAPTIST CHURCH, MOUNT VERNON, NEW YORK

*Nevertheless, we, according to His promise, look for . . . a new earth, wherein dwelleth righteousness.* II Peter 3: 13.

I am asking you to take a long look with me this morning. One of the dangers which I feel besets us is that often we are so intent upon examining the flower that we never see the garden; so busy are we in classifying the individual trees that we do not see the forest. The immediate task possesses us so completely that we never lift up our eyes to see the ultimate end of our efforts. The New Testament writers, however, never seem to have lost sight of the great goal towards which their efforts were tending.

The hope of a New Earth is one of the oldest that men have cherished. We endure the darkness of the night because we believe that the dawn will break. We fight with courage the hardest storm because we believe that on the farther shore are peaceful waters. Indeed, as one thinks of the progress which we have made, one questions whether humanity could have endured what it has endured had it not been for this power—psychological, is it? call it what you will—that comes from the thought that somehow the catastrophes or calamities or hardships of the immediate present are not in themselves permanent legacies which we shall carry all through life, but are the darkest hour which precedes the dawn.

A very striking example of this, I think, is the Great War through which we have so recently passed. There can be little doubt that one of the greatest powers which nerved the Allies, even in their darkest moments, was the hope that as a result of victory a new and better earth would be born. The events which have transpired since the signing of the Armistice may be tending to disillusion us somewhat; but as to the fact that we were inspired to fight and die, because we believed that Germany and the Central Powers stood between us and a better day, there can be little doubt.

It seems quite natural, therefore, that we should hear Peter speaking the way he does. Perhaps this was one of the things that inspired him, as it did so many of the other writers of the New Testament. How victoriously did they face the future! In the presence of the very worst that life held for them they still looked for a New Earth and spoke with confidence about it. Such was the hope of the early Christians and such must be our hope. We may differ with these men radically as to just how this new earth is going to come, but the fact of its coming should be just as real to us as it was to them. If we are to keep that courage, optimism, and triumphant faith which are the birthmarks of the Christian church, then we, too, must be able to look through the darkest night to the rays of the breaking dawn.

So much in a general way for the fact that the hope of a brighter future has always been and is to-day one of the chief sources from which we, as Christians, derive our power to press on. But now, more specifically, who is going to bring in this new earth? By what agency is it to be effected?

I suppose that one of the reasons for the courage and the optimism with which so many of the writers of the New Testament faced the future, was the fact that they thought that the coming of the new earth was something which was totally and entirely in the hands of God—that it was going to come in spite of human efforts rather than because of human effort. Sheltered beneath this protecting thought, they could look out upon the un-Christian conditions of their age and, as they saw the sky overcast by the clouds of sin, they could say with confidence: "Let the clouds gather. The time will come when God of His own self will break the clouds, the sun will shine again, the air will be purer, lo, a new earth will be born." There are still many people who think this. They speak with perfect assurance of the fact that we are now in the last dispensation and need to do nothing but wait for the catastrophic ending of the present age. But there are others who do not share this point of view, who, while they do not underestimate the tremendous part that God is playing in the bringing about of the new earth, nevertheless believe that human actions and human behavior bear a much more strategic and eternal relationship to the coming of the new earth than that of passing clouds which but temporarily veil the sun. These believe that if the new earth ever comes, it is going to come when men help God to bring it, or else it will not come at all. Now, if this is so, it is going to take more courage, and more faith, for us to believe firmly in the coming of the new earth than it did for these New Testament men, because from the vantage point of nineteen hundred years we see some things that they did not see, we know some things that they could not possibly have known. For one thing, we see that in addition to that implicit faith in God which they had, and which they handed down to us, we must add faith in man; and that is harder.

What does this mean for us? It means, first, that all human life assumes a new significance and takes on a new meaning. John Wesley tells us that once he went out into the fields and saw a group of Indians sitting by the bank of a river—there they sat. They spent their time in looking at each other, looking at the bubbles on the water, and looking at the sky. Except in time of war that was their occupation. What a life to live! I am wondering how they differ from us. How do we live? We eat and sleep, we work and play. Some of us think we would like to become rich and we get the mania for collecting money. Others of us want to become professional men and we go to college and get an education. And then what? Is that all? Are these things the ultimate ends of life? If they are, then we are at best but poor mortals following blind alleys which lead us nowhere. Christ says, "No." Life means more than that. We are laborers together with God, working with God, helping Him to bring in the new earth wherein dwelleth righteousness. We cannot possibly understand life apart from that great objective. Apart from that enterprise our lives are at best but beautiful bubbles which are blown up, display their colors to the sunlight and then break and are gone. But with that great objective life means something. We may feel that, like the thousands and thousands of little streams which are flowing from every continent, our lives are not isolated units wandering aimlessly. Like them we are all destined to find a larger and a fuller and a common life in the profundity of the ocean. With that great objective, everything that we do means something. Every unselfish deed, every act of sacrifice, every noble impulse that we obey, is not lost, but contributes towards that goal which is the end of all human effort—the building of a new earth wherein dwelleth righteousness.

So much for the fact that we are going to help

God bring in the new earth and that this adds new meaning to our life. Now there is another thought, and it is this: How is the new earth to come? There is difference of opinion here. I am one of those who believe that it is going to come slowly. There are many Christian people whose devotion and Christian enthusiasm we all admire, who think that the new earth is going to come just as suddenly as light which is ushered into a dark room when one presses an electric button. There are others of us, however, who think that it is going to come rather like the breaking of the dawn, at first but dimly seen upon the horizon and yet gradually but irresistibly throwing itself across the canopy of the sky, growing "brighter and brighter unto the perfect day." You and I shall not live to see the new earth in its entirety, but we are sowing what others shall reap just as we are reaping what others have sown. I have sometimes thought of the pioneer missionaries—Robert Morrison, who went to China; David Livingstone, who died in the dark heart of Central Africa; Adoniram Judson, who went to Burma—men who broke the virgin soil of the foreign field with their lifeblood. How discouraged they must have been! Think of Morrison as he met the stolid conservatism of that great nation who traditionally has harbored a spirit of fear, if not of antagonism towards the foreigner. He must have died feeling that he had accomplished little. And yet today China, whose doors had to be forced open, is of all nations most eager for the best that the West can give, and her young men are literally crowding our western universities. The pioneer missionaries did not live to see the new earth wherein dwelleth missionary activity, but they laid the foundations on which we have built. They sowed the seed which we are reaping. Others will reap what we are sowing. The writer of the Epistle to the Hebrews expresses the thought when, after having recounted the great Christian heroes and martyrs, he adds suggestively: "And these all . . . received not the promise; God having provided some better things for us, that they without us should not be made perfect."

We are going to help God to bring the new earth, and the new earth which is the Kingdom of God on earth, is going to come slowly. All good things come slowly. But I believe it will come, and my reason for believing that it will come is that other new earths have already come. As a matter of fact, the significant word in this text is not the word "new"; it is rather the word "righteousness." We have already had many new earths. Let me mention some of the new earths that have already come.

Commercial intercourse has given to us a new earth. There was a time when each tribe, each nation, used to think that it was the earth and lived in blissful isolation and ignorance of every other nation. Today the cords of commercial intercourse have tied up all the nations of the world in one big bundle, and we are either going all to swim or all to sink. Kipling somewhere compares the plying of merchant vessels between the western and the eastern hemispheres to the flying shuttle weaving the warp and the woof together into a world-wide industrial brotherhood. There are still many patriotic Americans who are reuttering the words of our forefathers to avoid "entangling alliances." We cannot do it. We are a hundred years behind the times. I shall never forget one of my professors in college when the War started. It was before America entered the War, and as he would take up the papers and read of the tragedies in Europe, with a smile on his face he would say: "Boys, I never was so thankful for the Atlantic Ocean as I am now." But it did not take him very long to find out that the Atlantic Ocean has been bridged; and, please God, it will remain bridged. Perhaps this was what President Coolidge had in mind when in his inaugural address he said, "The physical configuration of the earth has separated us from all of the old world, but the common brotherhood of man, the highest law of all our being, has united us by inseparable bonds with all humanity." The Atlantic and Pacific oceans have been bridged by these "inseparable bonds" of "common brotherhood" which are after all much stronger than any "physical configuration" which we may have. I grant you that we as a nation may disclaim all theoretical interest in European affairs. We may refuse to commit ourselves by treaty or any written document regarding our responsibility for or interest in the affairs of Europe. But as a matter of fact, we can no more avoid being shaken, and shaken violently, by European agitations than the peaceful harbor can avoid the angry surge of the boisterous ocean. Commercial intercourse has given to us a new earth wherein dwelleth mutual international dependence.

A new earth wherein dwelleth commerce, however, is not enough, for commerce has no soul. It has no predominating humanitarian interest. It is interested not primarily in people but in things. Its chief object is to make money. Hence, see England sending to the shores of the Orient the opium traffic—even when the Orient was trying to free itself from it. I understand, too, that the brewers of America are trying to establish in China the saloon which our country is attempting to drive out. No, a new earth wherein dwelleth commerce will not save us.

Democracy has given to us a new earth. No longer do we bow our heads to kings or follow blindly the dictates of those above us. Today every one of us, to a degree, has something to say as to how he shall be governed. Democracy has given to us a new earth wherein dwelleth, if even to a small degree, liberty, equality, fraternity. But a new earth wherein dwelleth democracy—in spite of the fact that we gave billions of dollars and millions of lives "to make the world safe for democracy"—will not save us. You know, as well as I do, that democracy is capable of being used in the hands of unprincipled men to perpetrate crimes which are just as horrible as were ever possible under the most autocratic system of government. If you think that any such catchword as "democracy" is going to save the world, you had better think more deeply. Give men freedom to act, the question still remains, What will they do? Give them opportunities for self-expression, the question still remains, What will they express? It doesn't need much argument to show that the form of government will always be subservient to the fact of life. Our freedom may mean for us true liberty or license. We may use it or abuse it. The choice which we make will be largely determined by our character. Democracy without character is a peril—we face it now. Democracy of itself will not save us.

Science has given to us a new earth. It has completely changed the face of the earth on which we live. A few weeks ago we all stood in silent admiration before that grand spectacle of nature, the eclipse of the sun, and our minds went back to the years gone by when people were afraid of eclipses. They would hide in their cellars, and others would shoot arrows at the monstrous dragon that was trying to devour the sun. Today, we read the heavens as we read a book. We can tell of all the movements of the stars and planets with just as much accuracy and precision as we can the movements of checkers on a checkerboard. We can talk to the ends of the earth. No longer do plagues wipe out, as they once did, vast civilizations, for science has taught us the secret of germ warfare. Science has given us a new earth wherein dwelleth knowledge. We know a lot. But a new earth wherein dwelleth science will not save us. Think of what science does in time of war! Listen to the words of a military scientist of the English-speaking race.

> Germ warfare [he says] was tried on a small scale during the late war, and its results have been promising. The method of its use was in poisoning water supplies with cholera and typhus germs, and the loosing of dogs inoculated with rabies into enemy country. Here at least is a promising beginning from which vast developments are to be hoped for.

That's science without God. If science has taught us anything, it has taught us the failure of mere knowledge to save the world. Indeed, one of the problems with which all thoughtful men who are concerned about the future of humanity are wrestling, is this, that our moral development is not keeping pace with our intellectual progress. We are discovering the secrets of science faster than we have the moral stamina to use them. It is like giving a child a loaded gun with which to play. Prof. James Harvey Robinson writes:

> Hobbes says of the scholastic philosophy that it went on one brazen leg and one of an ass. This seems to be our plight today. Our scientific leg is lusty and grows in strength daily; its fellow member—our thought of man and his sorry estate—is capricious and halting.

Will Irwin, in his book, *The Next War*, does not exaggerate the picture of destruction and death that awaits the human race if the next war comes. There will not be enough of us left to hold memorial services. All honor to science for what it has done to conserve human life, but science without God, without character, without the spirit of love, without righteousness, does become humanity's greatest enemy. Like fire it is a good servant, but a bad master. A new earth wherein dwelleth science will not save us.

My friends, the new earth that we need, and without which we perish, is the new earth wherein dwelleth righteousness. When will it come? It will come when we get in earnest about this matter. It will come when our Protestant denominations stop quarreling over nonsense, and, forgetting the petty things that separate us, unite together in one aggressive whole-hearted enterprise for the bringing in of the Kingdom of God. It will come when you laymen in our churches grow to see that the religion of Jesus

Christ is the most practical, common-sense thing in the whole world; when you will not be satisfied merely in keeping your religion in your hymn-books or Bibles, or within the walls of your church, but will take it out into the world of business and of politics, into all the avenues of life, and live it. It is about time we begin to take Christ seriously. We have been calling Him Lord, Lord, for many centuries, but in vain is all our avowed reverence if we do not the things that He says. Ships did not jump from lumber piles and launch themselves upon the ocean. Men made commercial intercourse possible. Democracy did not thrust itself upon us like sunshine after a night of darkness. Men thought enough of democracy to fight for it, to die for it, to live for it. Science did not just suddenly dawn upon us; hundreds of thousands of scientists have worked and are this moment working with almost superhuman effort in laboratories to make scientific progress possible. Why, then, should we think that righteousness is going to fall from the skies by some divine fiat? It just won't. God does not work that way. This new earth will come when we think enough of righteousness to take it out of the realm of theoretical appreciation and make it a part of all our human relationships; and if we do not do that, it will never come.

What kind of righteousness do we need? May I say, first, personal righteousness. For the individual who has not proved the supremacy of righteousness as a method of conducting his own life, will not want it for society or for the world. It is very easy in these days to say, "Lord, what wilt thou have the social order to do?" But that cannot take the place of the question, "Lord, what wilt thou have me to do?"

But personal righteousness, as important as it is, is not enough. We need to work also for social righteousness, because there is such a thing as social wrong. How shall we ever get social righteousness? For one thing, we shall have to be free men. This will mean that we cannot be Democrats all the time, nor Republicans all the time. It will mean that we shall not be forever condemning Labor as being radical and bolshevik in its attempts to better its conditions; nor shall we be forever accusing Capital of being the source of all the world's social ills. It will mean that we shall have to see the truth of what Abraham Lincoln had in mind when he said: "Stand with anybody that stands right. Stand with him while he is right, and part with him when he goes wrong." It will mean that we shall frequently have to knock the sides out of all the political, religious, and social man-made pigeonholes in which we are so often placed for classification. We shall not always be able to keep within vertical walls, but may have to walk horizontally across many fields. It will mean that we shall have but one obligation, that we shall be faithful to the one larger loyalty of following right as God reveals it to us, wherever it may take us, and whatever the cost.

But once more, we need international righteousness. Such mottoes as "Our country! . . . may she always be in the right; but our country, right or wrong," will have to go from our vocabulary and from our thinking. When our country is in the wrong, we shall condemn her for being in the wrong. We shall hate the wrong in our country as we hate it in every country, and we shall love the right in every country as we love it in our own country. Such mottoes as "America first" will have to go. There are some people who would try to make of America a great big hog with a long snout that noses all the little pigs out of the trough, and gobbles up the best for itself. I should be ashamed to be a citizen of such a country. "America first!" Yes, America first in her ideals; America first in her spirit of service; America first in her willingness to conserve those eternal principles of liberty, of brotherhood, and of equality which have ever been the charm of our country, and the vision of those who gave it birth.

This then is the task for which God wants us. "As laborers together with Him," He calls us to help Him in building a new earth of righteousness in ourselves, in society, and internationally. It is our task to help men and women to see that just as a large building is doomed to fall unless underneath it all, and through it all, and above it all, are those unseen but real bars of steel that hold it up, so all these great superstructures of man's imagination and of man's mind, commerce, democracy, science, and many others that we might mention, are doomed to destruction unless they are permeated by the spirit of righteousness. To conserve these great human values is our task for God and with God.

# IS JESUS STILL OUR SAVIOUR?

It is not the Cross that conquers; it is Jesus. The religion of Christ is no abstract thing, no mere system of dogma or ceremonial; it is life lived in the fellowship of Jesus, in devotion to his person, in loyalty to his cause. What this means in terms of personal experience, social ministry, and world affairs our younger men of the pulpit, of whom Mr. Stamm is a shining example, are seeking to interpret by every art at their command.

A Pennsylvanian, born in Millheim in 1883, Mr. Stamm prepared for college at the Fredonia Institute, after which he taught for three years in the public schools. Entering the sophomore class of Franklin and Marshall College, at Lancaster, he was graduated in 1907; taking his theological training in the Eastern Seminary of the Reformed Church, in the same city. He had three pastorates before he came in 1922 to Calvary Church, Reading, one of the leading parishes of the Reformed Church. He has contributed a number of very striking articles to the *Reformed Church Review,* as well as to the *Christian Century* and other journals.

The sermon following makes a sure appeal, by virtue of its forthright quality of thought and style, as of a man to whom Jesus meant what he said when he called men from their plausible prudences and hesitant assumptions to the great adventure of following his way of living. The pointed directness of the preacher, his urgent earnestness, his rich studentship and spiritual passion arrest and command us.

## IS JESUS STILL OUR SAVIOUR?

FREDERICK K. STAMM

CALVARY REFORMED CHURCH, READING, PENNSYLVANIA

*And thou shalt call his name Jesus; for it is he that shall save his people from their sins.* Matthew 1: 21.

Jesus comes to us, it has been said, "as one unknown without a name, as of old, by the lakeside, he came to those who knew him not. He speaks to us the same word, 'Follow thou me!' and sets us to the tasks which he has to fulfill for our time. He commands. And to those who obey him, whether they be wise or simple, he will reveal himself in the toils, the conflicts, the sufferings which they shall pass through in his fellowship, and as an ineffable mystery, they shall learn in their own experience who he is."

Our interest today is not in any of the ancient conceptions of Jesus, however well they may have served their age, but in his awakening of the soul to the presence of God. If we can get Jesus away from the false glamour of authority, out of stained-glass windows, out of our ecclesiastical twilight; if we can get him out of doors, out into the open fields, into the streets, where his influence will be unobscured by artificial masks; if we can look upon him as a real person, with a soul like ours, and listen to his words, not as spoken by an angel, but by a man whose chief interest lay in finding truth, I am quite sure his personality will have a better chance to operate, and our question will find a truer answer.

Jesus was here to be the achiever and doer of something that is eternally significant. We talk of him as a great teacher, a teacher of charm and insight, or a great example of idealism "who saw life steadily and saw it whole." He lived, some hold, the well rounded, rhythmic, poised life. "No," says Glover, "that was Sophocles." Here is a greater. He penetrates far deeper into things. He knows human nature, he knows the wrong that lies there, and the thing he means to do is to rid men of wrong and bring them back to God. It is not only a martyr's death toward which he is advancing. His step has in it a deep purpose. "I have a baptism to be baptized with," he says. "The Son of Man is come to seek and to save the lost." This brings us to the two great facts that are found in the text: Sin and the Saviour from Sin.

### I. SIN

I do not care by what name you call it—sin, evil, wrongdoing, missing the mark, or what not, this much I know: when a man gives himself over to an earnest study of God's ways in human affairs, and of God's laws and their working, the great contrasts in men's responses to God's rule become luminous. This contrast and this deflection from the will of God, I am pleased to call by no other name than sin. This is the shortest word, and carries with it as much meaning as any other.

I know of two ways whereby I can be made certain of sin. First, when I study myself. What is the use of inventing a theory of sin, when we find it in human life? It is an easy thing, too, to bring a charge of sin against humanity in general. "All have sinned and come short of the glory of God," says nothing. At least not enough to get under the skin of any one sinner and make him cry for forgiveness. Every one of our congregations will acknowledge sin in general without turning a feather. It means just as much and just as little as our syllogism in logic, "All men are mortal," which we all admit as a major premise, but which never makes us realize that we must die. I know sin when I know it about myself.

My own sin says three things to me. First, I have seen the better and done the worse. I know this not generally, but particularly and concretely. I take this ugly besetting sin of mine, which I have time and again dragged out into the sunlight and hewed to pieces, only to see it come to life again and dog my way. My experience tells me, also, that I have not only done evil, but I have liked it. I knew the warning against it, the appeal to everything worthy in me, but I did it. Ah, how I have liked it!

> What's done we partly may compute,
> But know not what's resisted,

says Burns. It is true. But the plea cuts both ways. I know "what's resisted." I also know the ideals of God that I resisted in doing the sin. But there is a third thing my sin says to me. Thomas Carlyle in Mrs. Austin's drawing-room, with "Sydney Smith guffawing," and "other people prating, jargoning, to me through these thin cobwebs Death and Eternity, sate glaring." "How will this look in the Universe," he asks, "and before the Creator of Man?" Yes, "But what will God say?" asks Browning in "The Worst of It." What will He say? God cannot regard us other than we are. When I sin my mind is clouded with the dark apprehension lest I should really find Him and He find me. My cry of "My soul is athirst for the living God; when shall I appear before the presence of God?" becomes the other cry of "Whither shall I flee before Thy presence?" I dislike the thought of God. I want to forget Him and everything that reminds me of Him. "Thus conscience does make cowards of us all."

I know sin because of a second thing. I see it about me, and when I see it, if I have any sense of right and wrong, I want to smash it. There stands the villainy of Iago. I've got to take a definite attitude of opposition against it. I cannot call it good. I must call it evil. And when I call it evil I mean that that kind of thing I am out against. If I am not out against it, what is the sense of calling it villainy? There is no such thing as thinking about evil in a disinterested frame of mind. Whoever thinks about it at all takes a definite attitude against it and cannot think about it on any other terms.

"Take this rule," said Susanna Wesley to her son John, "whatever impairs the tenderness of your conscience, obscures your sense of God, or takes the relish off spiritual things, that thing is sin to you, however innocent it may be in itself." Susanna Wesley was not a theologian. She was just possessed with a lot of common sense. Jesus did not define sin, but he did know that something "impairs the tenderness of the conscience, obscures the sense of God, and takes the relish off spiritual things." From this men must be saved. There is certainly a "push" for the souls of men from which Jesus would rescue them. There is some peril to which men are exposed, peril enough to make Jesus say, "I have prayed for you." And while Jesus did not define sin as did Susanna Wesley, he did illustrate it, which is far better. And if we want to preach to men, we must tell them as plainly as Jesus did what sin is.

Jesus said that sin is *hardness*. In the parable of the Last Judgment those on the right hand were instinctively kind, coming from the "overflow of the heart." Those on the left hand were instinctively hard. They committed nothing; they omitted everything that would provide a spiritual life for their fellow men. Such people Jesus warns. Jesus warned against the sin that was found in those people who would *like to do certain things if they could,* who at least are not unwilling to picture what they would like to do, if they could, and meanwhile enjoy the thought. They are not actual adulterers, they only wish they could be without being found out. They will not actually murder, but will not hesitate to wish that certain people were out of the way, and take great satisfaction in knowing that calamity has befallen their enemy. It is not only the act that Jesus condemns, but the color of the thoughts which dye and stain the mind.

Jesus said, too, that there were people who merely *played at religion.* They tithe anise and mint and cummin, and forget judgment, mercy, and faith. The Pharisee does not live in a real world. He makes a good appearance, but is more concerned with the cleanliness of the outside than with the heart out of which are the issues of life. He sets his prayers up as a smoke screen to his villainy. He does not devour more widows' houses than the Publican, but with this difference—the Publican does not tell himself any lies about it. The Pharisee has no God; he creates One, and the God he creates is quite different from the Reality. Against such trifling Jesus warned us. Bunyan sent Ignorance to hell. We do not like that term "hell," but where else was he to go? He would go there whether Bunyan sent him or not. Typhus germs send a man to death whether the physician wants him to go there or not. If a man jumps off a precipice he goes to destruction, and that is all there is to it. Why reason otherwise when it comes to the moral realm? It is not difficult to see why Jesus was so lenient with gross and flagrant sinners, and so exacting with Pharisees. The former certainly had need of God and they knew it. The latter, too, had need but were heedless of God's requirements.

Jesus finds the fourth kind of sin among those who never really *make up their mind*. Dr. Fosdick speaks of the "sin of the belated mind." Perhaps we have forgotten that Jesus said, "Thou shalt love the Lord thy God with all thy mind." "No man," he said, "having put his hand to the plow and looking backward is fit for the Kingdom of Heaven." This man is not bad. He is just "no good." He is static. The Kingdom of God is dynamic, and in the Kingdom of God there is no place for the nondescript. What part *can* there be in a Kingdom won on Calvary for people who cannot be relied upon, who cannot make up their minds and stick to it, or who cannot decide whether to plow or not to plow?

Does it make any difference to God what a man's

conduct is? If it does make any difference, and if there are certain things in the heart of man and in the universe, which God recognizes to be evil, how can that evil be turned into good, and from whence can a stream of purifying water be turned upon that putrid thing which threatens to destroy me?

## II. JESUS THE SAVIOUR

I lay it down as an axiom that Jesus is the Saviour, not because he was born of a Virgin, not because he performed miracles, not because he is the second Person in the Trinity, not because of any of these and many more reasons which the Church has given. But for far deeper reasons.

The first reason is, *that men have been changed.* When John the Baptist was languishing in prison, with waves of discouragement rolling over him, he sent and asked Jesus, "Art thou he that should come or look we for another?" Back came the answer, "The lame walk." That is reason enough. Since that time there have been many lame persons who were made to run without a limp. History is full of the record of the lives of such as these. There have been those who were *born* lame. There is in Jesus the power to rescue a man from the dead hand of ancestry. There was released in the world a power which each hard-pressed soul of man can lay claim to, as a power in his own behalf, and believe that if he find it, it is more forceful than all that is against it. Men have no longer need to say, "I have the moral defects of my father." There has been something that has come closer than the threatening of our natural blood; it is the spirit of Jesus.

There have been those who were lamed by *accident*. Some sin has made them hobble through life. Somewhere along their way they did something that was wrong. Something held them prisoner like Bonnivard in Byron's "The Prisoner of Chillon." He could hear the ripple of the waters of Lake Geneva, but he could not see them, for the only window in his cell was far away and far up. He became dead to the world; but one day a bird lighted on that window ledge and sang the sweetest song Bonnivard ever heard. It resurrected his dead heart. He longed to look into the face of his own native land. For days that grew into months Bonnivard dug footholes into the walls of his dungeon. Painfully, slowly, he climbed up, up, until at last his eye was on the level with the window, and he looked again into the face of the great mountains of Switzerland and upon the waters of blue Geneva. Up, up, men have climbed until they looked into the face of God in Christ and were satisfied.

Some have been lamed because they *would not walk*. They were too lazy to walk. This malady lies in the region of the will, and Jesus never compelled the wills of men. But we know something that changes the will. There is only one thing that can change a naturally lazy man—that is shame. He may become ashamed of himself when he looks about and sees others at work. This has been true spiritually. However men have sunk back upon themselves and excused themselves, the fact that one day they heard a far different call, made them ashamed of themselves.

Jesus is the Saviour of men, because he *shows us God*. He has no definition of God, but he assumes God, lives on the basis of God, interprets God; and God is discovered in his acts and relations. He said to Peter, "You think like a man, you don't think like God." Upon our idea of God will depend the kind of religion we have. "He that hath seen me, hath seen the Father." Not every one in Jesus' day saw Jesus. They heard him, they looked upon him, they saw his form, but they did not see *him*. Judas saw a man for whom he could bargain; Caiaphas saw a traitor to his country; the demoniacs saw a fiend who had come to torment them before their time; many of the Pharisees saw Beelzebub. We talk about the difficulty of seeing God; but we ought to talk about the difficulty of seeing Jesus. It is just as difficult to see Jesus as it is to see God. For nineteen hundred years Jesus has been trying to get us to see himself. We have sung about him, opened conventions and conferences in his name, but to do as he says, and to see as he sees, and to find God as he found Him, are quite other things. How shall we think about ultimate reality? What is back of all these changing, passing phenomena? Is anybody? If so, is he wise or blind? Is he good or evil or indifferent? Does He mean anything, or is He only unreasoning, purposeless force?

Well, this is what Jesus said: "Father." God, it has been said, "combines the strength and the tenderness, the authority and the devotion, the responsible control and the capacity for self-sacrifice which belong to Fatherhood at its best. Take the highest you have ever seen in fatherhood and raise it to the *n*th power, and then trust that, for that is God."

Jesus will still be the world's Saviour on condition that His conception of God as Father is preached and taught. He never spoke of a "pure doctrine," but of right practice and right living and right character. The great directing force in religion is a right vision of God, and if our vision of God is the vision of Jesus, then we shall be led in the right way. Perfect Fatherhood in God was the very heart of the Evangel of Jesus. To miss that is to miss Jesus. The great blot on the Church's escutcheon is the fact that the universal Fatherhood of God, and the universal brotherhood of man, taught by Jesus, have been put into the discard, and the religion *of* Jesus has been superseded with doctrines *about* Jesus. And the supreme crime of the world has been and is, not that it fails to be religious, but its failure to wipe out false pictures of God—of the warrior God, the unjust God, the hard God—and put in their stead Jesus' conception of God as Father.

Jesus is the world's Saviour only on condition that we heed his call to perfection and act on the belief that *he meant what he said.* Our difficulty is not to get people to believe that there is a God, and that Jesus lived and died. All this is assumed. But Jesus does not become the Saviour of the world merely because it is asserted that he is the Saviour, any more than water is life-giving without drinking it. What is the use of speculating as to the Saviourhood of Jesus unless there is a belief in the possibility of approximating to his perfection, and acting on the principle that he meant what he said?

In conversation some years ago with a woman on the subject of certain kinds of conduct, I told her that Jesus' ideals were thus and so. "But," she said, "Jesus was divine and we are not expected to be like him." Which was just another form of saying that for an idealistic religious genius those things are all right, but for the common man they are beyond reach. We so frequently hear it said, "Oh, he is an idealist," as though idealism were something beyond the average human range, not meant to be practiced, but to be talked about. Henrik Ibsen knew something about this when he wrote *Brand.* You perhaps recall the scene. It is in the first act. Brand is high up in the mountain snowfields. The mist lies thick and close; it is raining and nearly dark. A peasant and his young son are a little way behind. The peasant seeks to restrain Brand from going on because,

> "Here's an abyss that none can sound;
> 'Twill open and engulf us all."

But Brand goes on. The peasant thinks he is utterly crazy. But Brand turns to him:

> "Hear, Peasant; you at first professed
> Your daughter at the fjordside lying
> Had sent you word that she was dying,
> But could not with a gladsome heart,
> Until she saw you, go to rest?"
>
> "That's certain, as I hope for bliss!"
> "And at her last day mentioned—this?"
> "Yes."
> "Then come."
> "The thing's impossible—turn home."
> "Listen! Would you give twenty pound
> If she might have a blest release?"
> "Yes, Parson."
> "Forty?"
> "House and ground
> I'd gladly give away
> If so she might expire in peace!"
> "Would you also give your life?"
> "What? Life? My good friend—!"
> "Well?"
> "Nay, nay,

I draw the line somewhere or other—!
In Jesus' name, remember, pray,
At home I've children and a wife."
"He whom you mention had a mother."
"Aye, that was in the days of yore;—
Such things don't happen any more."
"Go home, you travel in death's track.
You know not God, God knows not you."

Yes, the things that Jesus said are either fine, high-sounding phrases, or else they are practical in their application. It is a dangerous thing to allow the sayings of Jesus to become mere platitudes constantly uttered from pulpits. "Be ye perfect, even as your Father in heaven is perfect," "Seek first the Kingdom of Heaven," "Do unto others as ye would that men should do to you" are frequently as meaningless to the present-day worshiper as they were to Tennyson's Northern Farmer:

"An' I never knowed what he meaned, but I thowt he 'ad summat to say,
An' I thowt he said whot he owt to 'a said, an' I coom'd awaäy."

Jesus may or may not be the Saviour of the world. It depends on the world. He may or may not be the Saviour of the individual. It depends on the individual. What right have we to talk about the Saviourhood of Jesus in the abstract? The condition of Saviourhood lies in this: Are we willing to pay the price? What privations men have suffered to get an education! There was Alexander Whyte, lodging with two others in a little room with a bed that could hold only two of them, so that they took it turn about to sit and work, four hours a shift, all through the night, paying about fifty cents per week for their garret and their food, and yet spending on occasion fifteen dollars for books, gathered from who knows where, and by what desperate privations! And if a man wants Christlikeness like that, he'll get it. You will not stroll into Christlikeness with your hands in your pockets, shoving the door open with a careless shoulder. Richard Cecil said, "You will not yawn yourself into heaven with an idle wish." It is a business for adventurous spirits. Let us cease our glib talk about a certain event on Calvary, and our singing,

> "Christ for the world we sing,
> The world to Christ we bring,"

until we are willing to say to men, "You can have Christianity only upon the same condition that you get other things—that you want it bad enough to pay the price."

Jesus is the Saviour of the world of men because he shows us what religion is by putting us into touch with the *Power that helps us do the thing we know we ought to do.* He who listens to the call "Follow me," must be prepared to follow him into some lonely places. To be saved means that when your path is beset by the fires of suffering and the shadow of death, you will not go round them but through them. There is an arresting passage in Mark's Gospel: "And they were in the way, going up to Jerusalem, and Jesus was moving on before them; and they began to wonder; and as they followed they began to be afraid." That's it. Even though you are afraid, are you loyal to the leader in front? Easy enough while the road runs by the shining shores of the Lake of Galilee, but not so easy when it turns into the Garden of Gethsemane and becomes the Via Doloroso.

A man's salvation is determined by what Jesus does for him. It is not so much a question as to his doctrinal beliefs, nor of what he should or should not do. He generally knows what he ought to do. He knows pretty well what his conduct ought to be. He knows what he ought to do when he is tempted to immorality, or to strike an enemy, or to drive sharp bargains. Not what a man ought to do, but how to get the power to do what he knows he ought to do. St. Paul's great statement, "I am not ashamed of the Gospel of Jesus Christ, for it is the power of God unto salvation," need not be clothed in a lot of theological speculation. As Dr. Jacks puts it in his book, *Religious Perplexities:* "I will base my life on the assumption that somewhere, in the height above or in the depth below, Power is waiting to back me up. That Power, if I find it, shall be my God." Let a man follow Jesus, and "he will reveal himself in the toils, the conflicts, the sufferings which they shall pass through in his fellowship, and as an ineffable mystery, they shall learn in their own experience who he is."

Who can tell all that is involved in getting the Power to do the thing we know we ought to do? Dick Blaisdell, in Albert Parker Fitch's novel, *None So Blind,* was a dissolute, drunken senior in college. He had a struggle with himself. He was telling his roommate of his last great battle with himself.

"Dick," said Phil, "I'm outside of it. I don't want to be, but I can't help it. I don't want to be fooled. How can you be so sure?"

"Because it happened, Phil. . . . Something that had been way down deep, rose up, rose up—nothing could stop it now—and took command. No power on earth could have taken me to the Reynolds after that. I stopped the boys. 'What's up?' said Bob. 'I'm not going any farther. I can't.' 'Can't?' said Atwood. 'You're never going to back out now!' 'I'm not backing out, I loathe it. I can't do it.' I turned round and ran for a car. After I started running, I just raced for it. I didn't notice what car it was. It landed me out in Brighton and I walked over here."

"Dick, if it was so real, why can't you give it to some one else?"

"I guess you can't ever do that with things that are real, Phil. I guess every man has got to get them for himself. Anyway, the fight's won."

This mystic element, this Power that makes for righteousness, this quest for reality, must be the experience of every man that is looking for the Power that is waiting to back him up.

We have said little about the cross, not because we minimize its significance, not because we want to get rid of it. You can't get rid of facts by saying you will get rid of them, any more than the Hindu priest could get rid of the germs of disease in the Ganges River by smashing the microscope. The cross is there. But you can't isolate it, and you can't see it set up by an arbitrary and omnipotent God. It was set up by men. Jesus could not escape it. He accepted it, and his acceptance of it is the crowning point in his victorious march. It is not the cross that conquers; it is Jesus. It is not a scheme, or a plan that we need, but a Person. It is not the *how* of salvation, but the personality to whom we are attached, a personality with a cross at its center.

"O Iole! how did you know that Hercules was a god?" "Because," answered Iole, "I was content the moment my eyes fell on him. When I beheld Theseus, I desired that I might see him offer battle, or at least guide his horses in the chariot-race; but Hercules did not wait for a contest; he conquered whether he stood, or walked, or sat, or whatever thing he did." How do we know that Jesus is the Saviour? Because he conquers whether he stands or walks or sits, or whatever thing he does.

# TRANSLATING THE GOSPEL

Dr. MacCallum is the twenty-third member of his family to be ordained to the Presbyterian ministry: so his fate was fixed. A Canadian by birth, he was educated at Queen's University, Kingston, and at Columbia University and Union Seminary, New York City, taking vows as a minister in 1903. After two brief pastorates he went to the Walnut Street Church, Philadelphia, where he has labored for fifteen years, busy alike in civic and church affairs. For years a contributor to the leading journals, such as the *Forum* and the *North American Review,* as well as to the church papers, he published his first book a year ago—*Now I Know,* a series of able essays in exposition of the basic truths of faith.

The sermon on "Translating the Gospel" is so finely conceived, so nobly uttered, so pertinent to the present plight of the world and the church, and withal so characteristic of a thoughtful and gracious preacher that it deserves a long pondering. No doubt there would be wide differences of view if everybody understood everybody else; but in a time torn by racial rancor and theological feud, it behooves us to consider how far the scattered mists of misunderstanding which gather into great clouds of controversy are due to a mistranslation of motives and ideas.

# TRANSLATING THE GOSPEL

JOHN ARCHIBALD MacCALLUM

WALNUT STREET PRESBYTERIAN CHURCH, PHILADELPHIA

*I heard a language that I understood not.* Psalm 81: 5.

Underneath this simple statement of fact there is an unsuspected poignancy of experience which relates the author to the thoughtful man of every age. The Psalmist is speaking for Israel in Egypt, but he is also expressing for us the disability we feel when we find ourselves in a situation where we cannot convey our ideas to others. Those who have traveled far afield know the embarrassment of being in a country whose language is unknown to them. This is a large part of the handicap suffered by the immigrant who comes to the United States from foreign lands. Being unable to tell of his needs, hopes, and fears, he is subjected to many a humiliation from which his native-born competitor is free. Much of the stupidity with which the so-called "alien" is charged is due to this inability to express himself. Like his prototype of old, the Israelite in Egypt, he is compelled to accept the most menial tasks—often to make bricks without straw—because he cannot speak the language of the country.

Much injustice has been done to the foreign-born through failure to take this handicap into account. Nor is this injustice confined to the ignorant policeman, yelling at the top of voice to the pushcart peddler, who stands before him dazed and confused, because he does not grasp his meaning. With much less excuse it has also been fostered by the scholar working in his psychological laboratory and drawing conclusions to support his bias in favor of the Nordic race from his intelligence tests. Forgetting that his own backgrounds are vastly different from those of the Russian or Roumanian peasant, he has given them examinations based upon his own rather than upon their experience, and then has condemned them to inferiority for being unable to meet an unfair test. As an illustration of this unfairness, we may take a picture problem in which the student is required to fill in an obvious lack in the picture. There is a tennis court with backstops, and two players with rackets in their hands and a ball upon the ground. How could any man who had never seen a game of tennis, even though he had the mind of an Aristotle, be expected to know that a net is lacking? Yet this is actually one of the tests which have been used to prove the stupidity of the non-Nordic alien, though his chief handicap is found in his lack of knowledge of the language which is rarely taken fully into account in these tests.

With the growth of civilization, the need of a

flexible means for the communication of ideas between those who speak different tongues is becoming more acute every day. Thus men of vision have dreamed for generations of a universal language. Esperanto was an abortive effort in this direction; it was too artificial to gain wide acceptance. Language is more than words, and besides there is not sufficient compulsion for the average man in any community to go to the trouble of learning such a system of communication even though it were practicable. Yet some way must be found to eradicate the misunderstandings which arise between peoples because of the barriers of different tongues. While it is true that one of the biggest factors leading to war is the collision of economic motives, this is greatly aggravated by the mutual misconceptions arising from the failure of nations to understand each other. War is much more apt to occur between peoples whose languages are different than between those speaking the same tongue.

These facts suggest the importance of the work done by the translator both in our own and past generations. He breaks down at least a part of the barriers between peoples, enabling them to catch glimpses of each other's virtues. He throws a bridge across the gulf between them, over which the more intelligent of his compatriots may pass to learn how akin the stranger is to themselves in his real nature. No man who has learned something of the mind of the Russian people through the translations of Pushkin, Tolstoy, Turgenev, Dostoevski, Gorki, and other writers of that nation, can have his faith in the ultimate destiny of the Russian people broken. He knows that they will eventually escape from the net of circumstance in which they are enmeshed at present. Having learned at first hand the greatness of the Russian soul, he is confident that it will rise again in self-expressive power and beauty.

A generation ago, the late William Archer introduced Ibsen to the English-speaking world through his masterly translations of the dramatic poet. Ibsen's message gave us a new understanding and appreciation of Scandinavian culture and thus tended to break down that inborn provincialism which narrows the horizons of all peoples; it also fell as a searchlight upon our traditional morality, prompting us to reëxamine the foundations of our social customs and sanctions, and thus led to the discovery of social shams of which we had previously been unaware.

No argument is needed to show that the work of the translator demands a high degree of skill. It is not enough to have an accurate knowledge of his own language and that in which the work he intends to translate is written. Every schoolboy who has tried to render a French story into English knows that often there is no exact equivalent for a French word in his native tongue. Though he searches his lexicon and grammar with all zeal, he soon discovers that there is something lacking in his rendering. It takes imagination to carry the author's meaning into another language so that it suffuses the new words which have now become the vehicle of his thought. Before this can be done we must not only know words in their combinations, but we must also be sensitive to their atmosphere. This explains why good translations are so rare. Sympathy with the author—the ability to catch the genius of his thought—is also essential, so that he who would convey adequately to his compatriots the message of a foreign author must have creative ability second only to the original writer.

Incidentally this explains the wonder and glory of the English Bible. Though it is a translation, or even in parts a translation of a translation of a translation, it has all the vividness and power of the original creation, because the men who rendered it into their native speech had, in addition to the essential intellectual equipment, the spiritual insight which enabled them to enter into its secret depths and draw forth its imperishable treasures. But a vital language is always in process of change, and often the men and women of today, when they read the majestic pages of the sacred writ, do not understand their meaning, for the literary language of the far-off days of King James sounds more or less remote and alien in their ears. This, to say nothing of the discovery of manuscripts which the translators of the Authorized Version did not have before them, or of advances in philology, justifies the making of new translations even though we still retain the familiar version in our devotions.

But this experience of the Israelites in Egypt has a much wider reference than to the spoken word. It is a symbol of most of the misunderstandings which mar the harmony of our human relationships. Deep in the heart of man there is an innate response to what is just and right. When a nation quarrels with its neighbor we are safe in the inference that both parties to the controversy are sincere, though each may be equally stupid or stubborn, and blind to the other's point of view. What is required in every such case is a translator, who, standing above the prejudices of both, will be able to interpret each to each. Most of our demands are subject to modification when we see the reasons which explain our neighbor's difference from us. When two people who have quarreled are wise enough to have a friend arbitrate their disagreement, neither is likely to be found blameless.

One of the most prolific causes of misunderstanding in our current life is that due to the fact that different parties in the Christian church do not know each other's speech. There is not an unbridgeable abyss between the religionist and the scientist, or between the fundamentalist and the modernist. Their mutual hostility can be accounted for by their failure to understand each other's intention. The most advanced of the higher critics will not admit that he holds the Bible in less esteem than his fundamentalist neighbor. But the latter cannot follow him. He thinks that his mental processes are out of gear, that he is spiritually perverted. On the other hand the modernist is convinced that the fundamentalist is confusing the essence of the Bible with the local and temporary modes of expression used by the Spirit of Truth in each period of biblical history. The one interprets, or believes that he interprets, the Bible literally, the other freely. Neither does the other justice, though the fundamentalist is usually more severe in his censure because he believes his opponent to be morally culpable, whereas the modernist only regards the fundamentalist as militantly ignorant.

This failure to understand the languages of the two dominant parties of the present-day church has resulted in disastrous consequences. Thousands of young people have lost interest in organized religion because of the squabbles of the theologians. In multitudes of cases instead of taking sides, they say, "A plague on both your houses." Meantime the cause of Christ languishes and evil remains unchecked because the forces of good are divided. What is required on each side is a greater patience in learning the other's tongue. When a man insists that his neighbor shall explain his religious experience in the same terms that he himself uses, he is like a German who insists that his French neighbor shall speak German. This may be difficult or even impossible, to say nothing of its being unreasonable. Above all, men must learn to trust each other, and have faith in each other's purity of purpose or there will be friction, embarrassment, weariness, and cynicism. But where there is mutual forbearance, supported by a will to reciprocal fairness, misunderstandings are certain to dissolve into the light of common day.

In our modern life, the ancient controversy between science and theology still goes on and often is bitter in tone to the spiritual disadvantage of both parties, since true religion cannot thrive in an atmosphere of hostility and recrimination. Here again, the underlying cause of the disaffection is the difference of language. The scientist deals in facts and is not primarily interested as a scientist in their influence upon religious and other dogmas. The geologist sinks a shaft into the earth to lay bare its various strata that he may read at first hand the successive chapters in the story of its development. He naturally resents the aspersions upon his integrity or ability which are so often made by the spokesmen for religion, who do themselves injustice because of their fear that he will undermine the foundations of their inherited beliefs. Fear is the most cruel of the affections, and one of the quickest to becloud the mind and impair the validity of its judgments. Misinterpreting the motive of the scientist, and failing to appreciate the fact that truth is always the ally of a healthy faith, most of the leaders of religion have continually attempted to block the traffic in new ideas and forms of thought. The pioneers of science in their impatience and exasperation have often allowed themselves to deny the unquestionable values the religionist was trying to conserve and the progress of the Kingdom of God has been sadly retarded. They have lacked the sympathy which should have marked men of their breadth of outlook. The long, sad story of the conflict between the exponents of the religious and the scientific aspects of truth could have been almost entirely avoided if each had understood the other's language.

It must be remembered, however, that every man is a unique creation and therefore has the intrinsic right to self-determination within the ineluctable limits set by the common welfare, so that honest differences of opinion upon each and every possible question will always remain. This accounts for the tendency of every group to organize into at least two parties, each of which gathers around a nucleus which is polaric to the other. Thus if any like-minded group, whether fundamentalist or modernist, is relieved from external pressure and allowed to go its own way, it soon develops internal differences of opinion. This is a sign of health and is in accordance with the laws of human existence. When the

Old and New Schools of the Presbyterian Church in the United States united in 1870 after a cleavage of a generation, many representatives of the Old School were more progressive than some of those of the New. The conservatives of yesterday had developed their own liberal party, while both schools had passed beyond the issues upon which they had separated, over thirty years before.

If these basic psychological facts could be kept in mind, the resultant insight would act as a lubricant by which many of the frictions of life would be avoided. Nor, as we have seen, is this idea of lingual separation confined to religion. The misunderstandings of youth and age, of capital and labor, of party and party, of temperament and temperament, however impassable they appear, can be at least partially bridged in our present state of imperfection if both parties recognize as their first duty the learning of the other's point of view. Even where the originating cause of the difference is a conflict of economic interest, a common language will go far to allay suspicion and make agreement possible.

I have no intention of suggesting that a universal medium of expression would banish sin from the world. Only God in the hearts of men can do that. There are those who see the light and yet disobey it in their lust and greed. But even in many such cases their course would be different if they knew what they are really doing and recognized the rights of those over whom they are ruthlessly trampling, or whom they are exploiting. But enough has been said to indicate the necessity of our working zealously to build highways of understanding in order to unite those who by birth, training, or education, look upon their fellow men who are equally virtuous and sincere, as the enemies of their faith and ideals. We must establish a concordat among all who believe in God and seek to do his will and find in Christ the way of salvation. The story of Babel reveals and illustrates the cross purposes and confusions that arise when men are unable to understand each other. Unity of action among men of high ideals can be secured only when they have learned to recognize how superficial are their differences and how fundamental are the agreements which underlie their variations in accent.

If these reflections are sound, it is evident that the man of high character will always be on the alert to break down the walls of prejudice and misunderstanding which separate different groups and result in violent animosities. But since man derives from God, it is not surprising to find that this is what God is always doing. He strives with his children continually to teach them his thought and purpose. It is not enough that his revelation should be written in a sacred book: it must be translated into terms of life—into breadth and thought and deed. The leaders in the kingdom of heaven are those who are establishing a new understanding of God by the beauty of their lives and the persuasive witness which they give to the truth they have experienced.

Nor is it an easy thing to learn the language of God and then to teach it to others who do not comprehend its vocabulary. Before the phrase "Love your enemies" can be translated into a habit, there must be a long, hard course of discipline; but none who has ever taken that course has failed to find unmeasurable profit in it. To know another language enlarges and enriches the mind. But to know God's speech and make it known to others is life eternal.

God's speech? "The Word was made flesh, and dwelt among us (and we beheld his glory, the glory as of the only begotten of the Father), full of grace and truth." The greatest social tragedy is the fact that there are so few who know this language. None indeed dare claim to have mastered it so as to have grasped fully its rare suggestiveness, its clarity of definition, its inexhaustible depth of meaning, its glorious promise, its unfailing power to inspire and redeem. But the fact that there are so many millions in this and other lands who hear this language yet know it not, places upon those who comprehend it though only vaguely, and speak it with stammering tongue and faltering accent, the solemn obligation of translating it into terms that the multitudes can understand. And what are those terms? Not any that can be set forth in lexicon and grammar and other repositories of philological lore, but in kindness of attitude, in breadth of sympathy, in generosity of impulse, in nobility of character. Christianity at last must stand or fall, win or lose in its contest for the spiritual sovereignty of the world, by the success or failure of those who bear the name of Christ in commending themselves to every man's conscience in the sight of God. Probably the most painful aspect of organized Christianity is the fact that our dialect is so provincial and our accent so strange that so many of the aliens among us do not know that we are trying to tell them of the unsearchable values of God in Christ. Presbyterian, Episcopalian, Methodist, Baptist—these words are only jargon to the widow in the Ghetto, or the Polish mother distraught by the impossible task of bringing up a large family respectably in two rooms in a land where every one outside of her narrow circle looks upon her with level eye. But there is a language that both of these women can easily learn—a language that will melt their hearts and quicken their latent goodness into a serene and seasoned faith in God and man—the language of sympathy, kindness, helpfulness, and love, as incarnated in Christ. The sublime and inspiring task of those who know this exalted tongue is to translate its message into such simple terms that the humblest alien cannot say of the churches of America, "They speak a language that I know not."

Recently a gifted scholar and saintly character

died in London where for many years he had made his home. Baron von Hügel was an Austrian by birth and a Roman Catholic in religion. But he mastered the tongue of the country of his adoption so that he was able to understand the people among whom he lived. He was a student of religion who found no conflict between science and higher criticism on the one side, and an exalted devotion to Christ and his church on the other. There was no provincialism in his outlook. He was always ready to address Protestant religious gatherings whether of laity or clergy and to read with eagerness and profit the writings of Protestant scholars. He presented the spiritual treasures of the ancient church in such terms that they took on a universal meaning, and at his touch the jealousies and suspicions which are rife on a lower plane vanished from sight. It is safe to predict that when the day arrives that the catholicity of temper and breadth of outlook of Baron von Hügel are representative of the leadership of the Christian churches, the new earth of the apostles' vision will be here. Meanwhile, our task is to learn the language of those who do not understand us, that like this noble scholar we may translate the gospel of Christ's emancipating grace into deeds of such loveliness, beauty, and truth that they will understand, and fear and suspicion will be banished from their hearts.

# VISIBLE AND INVISIBLE

From the priesthood of the Roman Church to the pastorate of a Unitarian Church is a long leap, albeit in a line of straight thinking, all depending on whether we find the source of religious authority embodied in the Church without or enthroned in the spiritual reason within. None the less it is a romance, and one feels the stress and strain of the struggle as Dr. Sullivan relates it in his remarkable *Letters to Pius X*, published in 1910, to which ought to be added, as companion volumes, *The Priest* and *From the Gospel to the Creeds*—three most illuminating books.

A native of the Old Bay State, Dr. Sullivan was educated in Boston Theological Seminary and the Catholic University. Ordained to the priesthood in 1899, he served in the fellowship of the Paulist Fathers, and for seven years was a teacher of theology in Washington. In 1909 he joined the Unitarian Church, and held pastorates in Schenectady and in All Souls Church, New York City, until 1923, when he became mission preacher under the auspices of the Layman's League. He has recently settled again in the pastorate, in the Church of the Messiah, St. Louis.

Some of us regard Dr. Sullivan as one of the really great preachers of our time, not alone for his fine intellect and his literary grace, but because something of the mysticism of his Catholic background and training touches and transfigures his wide-ranging liberal thought—a union of qualities rare enough and still more rarely blended. In the sermon following we see a noble intelligence moving in a large orbit, making the august reality of an Unseen order real, commanding, and consecrating.

## VISIBLE AND INVISIBLE

WILLIAM L. SULLIVAN, D.D.

CHURCH OF THE MESSIAH, ST. LOUIS

*Blessed are your eyes, for they see.* Matthew 13: 16.

It is but a matter of course to say that in this sentence Jesus did not refer to physical seeing. If we have eyesight at all, we must see by an inevitable and automatic act; and to the inevitable and automatic no blessedness belongs, and none is promised. The seeing referred to here is not donated but won; is not physical but spiritual and personal; is not a capacity for knowing the things of the material world, but a power for beholding the Reality that sustains the universe of souls. The first principle of religion is that such a Reality exists; the first commandment of religion is that we discipline and perfect ourselves for seeing it; and the first warning of religion is that we may by indolence or coarseness lose the vision of it, and by losing it, lose the happiness, the fulfillment, and the peace that should be the portion of our spirits and the purpose of our lives.

Now as soon as we say that there is a world of reality invisible to the physical eye, and beyond the power of any other physical sense to perceive, a prejudice is likely to arise in the mind of the "practical man," as the saying is. He at once puts himself on guard. He fears being overreached and deluded. He has a just dread of imaginative misleading and sentimental hallucination. He believes that his daily life and experience are carried on in the midst of tangible things which control him more than he can ever control them, and he suspects the existence of any order of being not capable of definition in their terms or of portrayal in their likeness. In this interpretation even of the world around him and of his own daily deeds, he is in error, for these too we shall see are established upon the invisible.

Let us, however, frankly admit the amount of truth that this prejudice contains. There is a world invisible and mankind has always been invincibly persuaded of it. But what is a great part of the history of mythologies and theologies but an effort to compromise it by defining and describing it falsely? Imagination and reason when ignorantly and perversely exercised upon it have deluded millions by vain devices, desolate superstitions, cruel and immoral teachings. Thus religions, by materializing the pure essence of spiritual wisdom and by trying to confine it within the transient dialect of one age, have made men doubt that since so many presentations of the divine reality are false, any presentation of it is true. Religions have in this manner lost their authority, not by insisting upon their unseen foundation, but by departing from it; that is to say, by the vain attempt to shut up the eternal in a temporal definition and to exhaust the spiritual in terms of sense and material imagination. So much of truth there is in the practical man's distrust, whenever such phrases as "the invisible universe" are spoken in his ears.

We shall, however, keep in mind that no institution or ideal could survive if it were judged only by the excesses committed in its name. Liberty lives although many of those who profess to love it most have profaned it worst. So, despite the violence done to the soul's supreme ideal by many who have claimed to speak for it, religion is and forever will be; its essential assertion of unseen Reality stands immovable and sure; and the blessedness promised by the greatest of its teachers to the inward vision that discerns it is every day bestowed.

Let us approach this existence of the great Glory and Transcendence by observing how much in the ordinary life of men belongs to the invisible. The extent of this it may surprise us to discover; and the realization of it may help us to understand the deepest principle both of philosophy and of religion; namely, that the world which appears to our senses is rooted in a Life and Power that can be seen only by the spirit.

Our first instance will be the moral ideals of mankind. Truth is one of these. Truth by the noblest of our race has been loved and adored. Men have accepted poverty in order to serve it; they have given themselves over to loneliness and friendlessness in order to be loyal to it; they have trudged forth into exile, have died in prisons and in flames in order to protect it and in pure and selfless faithfulness to minister to it. If anything in this world is real, it is Truth; if anything has authority, Truth has it; if anything commands and blesses life, Truth does, as a cloud of witnesses bears testimony. Yet from every sense that perceives the world of things it is utterly hidden. No retina pictures it, no hands touch it. Neither can any space confine it, nor any era of time contain it. It is timeless, therefore eternal. It is in no "here" and "there" as bounded objects are, but belongs to an order of existence to which our limiting sense-words of "here" and "there" or "now" and "then" do not and cannot apply. Yet we know it and aspire to it. But if we do, it is because we have a vision that is not of the earthly eye, and a world to live in that is not of material measurement. And so it is with every ideal of the soul. Justice is the foundation of states, the coercive authority of righteous law, the glorious and awful imperative that governs our relations to others. Anything more real and practical we can hardly imagine. Anything closer to the structure of our souls we cannot discover. Anything more important for human life, and so completely impossible to dispense with we could not find on earth. Yet who has seen Justice? No one has seen it except with the eye that beholds the things of the spirit, that sense within whose field of vision is the super-sensible and everlasting.

Now let us descend to an area of experience which seems to be tangible, visible, alive with color, and quick with movement. This is History. "What!" we may say. "Do you mean that there is anything invisible in history? Why, the very condition of its being history is that it is acted out in the earthly arena of this solid world. Kings and courts, treaties and constitutions, the march of armies and the din of battle, the sailing of seas, the migration of peoples, jurists, prophets, poets, cathedral builders—the whole enormous transaction is a spectacle and pageant. How can the invisible be attributed to it or it to the invisible?" So runs the protest of the natural man. And yet the forces that create history, the powers that set that spectacle and pageant in motion, are in their turn invisible. For history is made by human motives and ideals. Hope, fear, ambition, zeal, faith, liberty, aspiration—these it is that speak the creative word and call into existence armies and colonies, laws and constitutions, and the whole sadness and splendor of our human story. Here too that which appears is rooted in a reality that to the outward eye and pictorial imagination does not appear.

A similar truth holds even with science. Science

deals at last with forces and with laws. Science knows no inert or isolated thing. Everywhere to science is the play of energy, everywhere are attraction, repulsion, composition, disintegration, ever and forever active. These activities constitute the world and the essence of things. Things in activity, then, things manifested by force, are the objects of science. Yet what is force? It is something that in itself is invisible. Our great earth swings in space round the sun. Nothing visible holds it there. So far as our senses can see there is between us and the sun only emptiness, and all above us and all beneath us, emptiness. In majestic constancy our earth keeps its orbit by virtue of a power that we call gravitation. We know nothing of gravitation, nothing of the mystery of that "attraction" that is exercised in a fixed ratio according to distance and mass. We can give it a name, but we can do no more. "Energy," "Force," "Law"—these certainly designate reality; they are the very field of science, the reason why there is and can be such a thing as science. They are not, however, given to the senses, but are devised and constructed by the pure intellect. Science at every step deals with the invisible. Physics cannot draw a breath without implying metaphysics.

One final example which perhaps may strike you as the strangest of all. We are invisible to one another. You do not, and in this life at least, never can see me who stand before you. What you see is a composition of matter called a body. This body you perceive making motions that reach your eyes and setting up other vibrations in the ether, if there is an ether, that reach your ears. But this material compact, this piece of external matter, which is the closest to us of all similar physical substances in the world, this thing called body—is not you or I. For we are first and foremost not things but persons. As persons we are constituted not of molecules but of motives, beliefs, virtues, the purposes of our wills and the thoughts of our minds. And these realities, this essence of ourselves, no one outside us can ever see. We may reach them by more or less accurate inference from deeds done and words spoken; but immediately see them in any one else we cannot. The world of persons is a world invisible.

These considerations rather humble us. We had fancied that the far-flung bulk and magnitude of the world gave its secret away at once; that it was all there, awaiting only eyesight to be read to the end of the chapter. But this, we begin to understand, is an illusion. The world indeed is there; if we like to say so, it is all there. But it takes more than eyesight to learn the story spread upon that mighty page. Without the power of seeing by the spirit, our faculty of seeing merely by the eye would never give us knowledge. The least learned as well as the most learned of us in every operation of the intelligence and every act of conscience, displays insight into a non-material world the realities of which give basis and meaning to the material world we see. When we realize this we are no longer humbled by the limitations of our organs of sense; but we are lifted up first to wonder and then to worship by the thought of our intellectual and moral grandeur as we pass beyond the barriers of the physical and temporal and come near to the Thought and Mind which informs and sustains the universe and has made us kindred to Himself.

Religion means taking this step to wonder and worship. Just as there is no understanding the material without our presupposing the non-material; just as the physical universe could never give us knowledge unless the pure intellect interpreted it as "cause," "law," "energy," and other such non-physical realities; just as there is no knowing the man we see with bodily eyes until we perceive his motives, purposes, and thoughts which no bodily eyes can discover; so, says Religion, if you would reason out the meaning of an existence thus based upon the invisible and if you would comprehend the value, worth, and splendor revealed in that existence, you must rise to the single Source of both the existence and the value, a sovereign Transcendence, whom we name Creator and Heavenly Father. In Him the invisibles meet and find their origin and rest. Where but in His supreme Reason can the reason in the universe, which science is ever finding to be of more and more majestic harmony, find a possible foundation? Where but in His Holiness can the ideals that command us with an intrinsic authority be given a place in the universal life? Unless the universe is marvelously successful at its lowest—in molecules and atoms and juices and gases—but desolately bankrupt at its highest—in souls, ideals, and aspirations—then the crown of existence and the destiny of our souls is God.

But religion goes farther than this. It does not merely present us with an argument. It invites us, it dares us, to put its principles to the test of experience. Try it, says Religion. Look upon the universe as having no spiritual origin or home for souls. Regard souls, the highest thing we immediately know, as being produced by something that had not any soul. Make the effort to consider the universe a gigantic heap of material fragments, as destitute of a mind as a bleached skull is of a brain. Behold that vast mass of magnitudes and forces as unstirred by spirit, although you, one speck and atom of it, have, in mind and conscience, something which the whole rest of it has not. Try to live the highest life of reason, of character, of aspiration, of nobleness, upon that basis. Try to reconcile these shattering contradictions, and to live in this essential spiritual isolation from the universal life that produced you. Then when you have wearied of it, as beyond any doubt you will, provided you cultivate all your noblest powers, make experiment of the other principle. See the visible as set in the invisible. Look upon the world as thought unfolding according to the law of advancing perfection. Consider soul, the highest reach of the process in our ken, not as a by-product, but as organically belonging to the Power that moves the mass. Consider that the universe is not so paltry as to have room for solids and liquids but no room for souls. Estimate the spirit's aspiration as a higher form of energy and of more deep significance than any other. Know that when standing at the summit of your thought and sending your vision into the heart of reality, you are not met by the blank look of the forever dead, but are answered with the radiant countenance of the forever living. Elevate your natural gifts of wonder, trust, aspiration, to their congenial end and object. Do not separate yourself from humanity, but unite yourself to all our race at its highest, as it has adored in life and shown trust and hope in pain and death. So live, and then answer which conception thus experimentally tested, fits a universe of order and answers to the nature of your spirit. You will find that in the one case your soul is broken and frustrate, and in the other, fulfilled and perfected. You will learn that the more we know of spirit, of the depth and height of personality, the more clear is it that spirit and personality are the key to all existence, the assurance of the reality of all ideals, and the only promise of fulfillment in the immense evolution yet to be.

When in this way we see and verify in ourselves the promise of blessedness given to the seeing, old words long known to us are illuminated and enlarged with a new majesty. Truth becomes God Almighty progressively revealed to the mind. To violate it by living a lie is seen to be calamity and the ruin of our essential souls. Justice becomes the One who inhabiteth eternity progressively revealed to Conscience. To profane it for the transient phantom of selfish gain or power is perceived to be a devastation greater than if the constellations dashed about in chaos. Pure love and noble loyalty become rooted in the Lord and Father of souls progressively revealed to the heart. To defile them is known to be collapse and death. But to strive in our mortal day to make these mighty realities visible to the eye within, and to rise by our service of them to the contemplation of the adorable and eternal Life who is their foundation, this is the blessedness of union and communion with God. These are the eyes that are blessed because they see.

Consider the progress of man on his way to this mount of vision. How many a man has tried to serve his party or his sect by falsehood, and not known that he is falsifying, for he covers his transgression by an ignoble use of a noble word—loyalty! For years he may so go on, with veracity and equity all the time disintegrating. By the habit of subtle reticence, of cunning phrase, of evasive suggestion, he unfits himself to be a servitor of Truth. By an infection of the eye of conscience he sees his party interests large, and the pure presence of the Truth which is above all our factions, dim and small. He knows that he must serve his group; he does not yet know that he must make this service subordinate to the service of the most high God. If ever he casts a look that way he shrinks and is afraid; for the path seems sometimes lonely to those who have not yet found in the great Companion comradeship enough. So all round the eyes of this man of our example are held. He does not see.

But on one day, forever to be remembered in his life, he is made to see. In some quiet hour of reflection or in some crisis of decision, the walls of his captivity fall down; prejudice and partisanship which were so solid become unsubstantial; the disorder which had caused a lesser loyalty to thrust out the greatest takes its true proportion; the Seeker and Illuminator finds him and gives him sight. He sees at last, and blessed are his eyes. A sovereign Authority and immortal Beauty are realities to him now, and never again, whether he lives or dies, can he be of set purpose faithless to the light that shines from the God who is Truth. Of this great process he cannot give you a detailed account. There is no chain of discoverable logic linking the beginning of the change with the end of it. Purely and simply he that was blind now sees. He is awakened; he is recreated; he that was the servant of phantoms becomes a free son of the Only Real.

A tremendous hour in life it is when by some such direct communion we know Him who is our End. Then not by hearsay, but by experience we make acquaintance with the Lord of the world invisible, and through our mortal twilight see Him with an inner sense that He has touched and quickened. Sure is the promise; let us work to realize and deserve it: "Blessed are your eyes, for they see."

# BAPTIZED FOR THE DEAD

America is deeply in debt to Scotland for the number of good and great preachers it has sent to our shores, some of them coming as young men and growing up among us, while others have come in later life. To repeat their names would be to write a roll-call, highly honorable alike to the land of Burns and the land of Lincoln. Our Scottish brethren unite three rare qualities which go to the making of a preacher—fine scholarship, fearless thinking, and a deep and sincere piety.

Among those who have brought us these gifts is Dr. Mutch, a native of Aberdeenshire and a graduate of Edinburgh University, where he took both his Arts and his Divinity courses. His first appointment after being licensed to preach was Assistant Minister of the West Church of St. Nicholas, Aberdeen, where he served two years, when he was elected and called to the pastorate of the West Church of Galashiels. There he spent four years, and was then called to the Parish of Muthill, near to the Trossachs, in Perthshire, and after ten busy and fruitful years was invited to the Presbyterian Church of Bryn Mawr, Philadelphia, in succession to Dr. Johnston Ross.

A busy pastor in a noisy age, undisturbed by the issues now agitating the church—having faced those questions years agone—Dr. Mutch maintains a high tradition of leadership in a college community, by virtue of his genius as a preacher, his skill as a pastor, and, by no means least, the great personal affection which he inspires. The Hallowtide sermon is typical of his work, in its simplicity of structure, its wealth of illustration, its evocation of the religious atmosphere, and its practical appeal; a sermon of a kind too rare among us, expounding one of the greatest phrases of the Creed: "I believe in the Communion of Saints."

though that be so, Hallowtide is a festival that cannot but appeal, reminding us, as it does, of all those who have passed on, not only the great and famous, but also the "unknown good." The late Principal Forsyth of Oxford used to speak of "the Great Church," not of any one denomination, but the Great Church, great enough to be the True City of the Living God. But we have only a very poor conception of that grand fellowship if we were to leave out of sight the ever increasing part of it which is gathered on the farther shore.

One family we dwell in Him;
One Church, above, beneath;
Though now divided by the stream—
The narrow stream of death.

Stephen Graham, in writing of the Russian piety, tells of a remarkable Communion custom. He says that at each Communion time, the worshipers purchase a little loaf at the porch of the Church, and send it with a piece of paper to the priest at the Altar. On the piece of paper are written the names of fathers, mothers, grandparents, children, and friends. The priest receives all the bread and the papers, and then in the silence before Mass is celebrated, he reads out the names. The stranger would not know who were living, and who were dead, and it gives a sense of fellowship with the whole family in heaven and on earth. And that is part of the message of Hallowtide. In the communion of believing souls there are no dead.

Saints of the early dawn of Christ,
  Saints of Imperial Rome,
Saints of the cloistered Middle Age,
  Saints of the modern home;
Saints of the soft and sunny East,
  Saints of the frozen seas,
Saints of the isles that wave their palms
  In the far Antipodes.

Saints of the marts and busy streets,
  Saints of the squalid lanes,
Saints of the silent solitudes,
  Of the prairies and the plains;
Saints who were wafted to the skies
  In the torment robe of flame,
Saints who have graven on men's thoughts
  A monumental name.

*Then, a second Hallowtide truth, enshrined in our text, is that of "others who have labored and we have entered into their labors."* You are all aware of the deep longing and earnest desire on the part of dying men that their work should be carried on and completed. They have been standard bearers in some great cause, and they are anxious that others should seize the flag as it falls from their dying grasp. George Eliot has pictured that hunger of the human heart with a tender touch in two of her stories. You have read *Romola*, and you recall how the aged philosopher, Bardo, feels life oozing out of him. Every day his body grows frailer, and his mind less acute. But he delights in the manly strength of his son, Dino, and rejoices in the fond hope that his son will take up the glorious task that he has to lay down. And the old man's grief is terrible when Dino refuses the charge and leaves his father to die without a successor. Then in contrast to that tragic story, there is *Daniel Deronda*. And you remember the unbounded delight of the aged Jew when he found that Daniel would echo his voice, and continue his work after he was gone. And so it is. It is good for a man to make his will, to leave all his affairs in perfect order, and to die with no anxiety concerning things in this world or the next. But that man can greet the Angel of Death with a radiant smile, who can point to another, youthful, strong, and enthusiastic, who will grasp the tools that fall from his hands, and carry on his good work to completion. That man rears his own immortality, who has his spiritual successor "baptized for the dead." And so often has it been.

> Out of sight sinks the stone
> In the deep sea of time,
> But the circles sweep on.

Take John Wesley. Strictly speaking, he was a childless old man when he died. Yet we all know that the Sons of John Wesley form a host which no man can number. Indeed, it is often the case that the best work of a great soul is not done by himself in his own person or lifetime, but by those who were baptized for him, and took up his great cause. And I think of two missionary records. There were two brothers, Thomas and William Knibb. Thomas was apprenticed to Mr. Fuller, the friend of William Carey, and from him he caught the missionary enthusiasm, and afterwards sailed for Jamaica. He landed in January, 1823, but died within three months. And when the sad news reached home, William, the younger brother, was so impressed by the pathos of it all that he begged to be allowed to go in his brother's place, and take up his brother's task. And he went. William Knibb was baptized for his dead brother, and became the great missionary to the people of the West Indies. Similarly in the days when Thomas Chalmers was rousing the Church of Scotland to her duty to the heathen world, a young man named John Urquhart was powerfully affected by the burning passion and resistless logic of Chalmers's plea. And he volunteered to carry the Gospel to India. But he died before he had even started. He had a bosom friend, Alexander Duff. They were as brothers. Duff had never thought seriously of Missions, but he was deeply moved by the thought of his great friend's lofty purpose and tragic end. He hurried home and told his parents what had happened and asked permission to take up Urquhart's cloak. That consent was given, and Duff went to India in Urquhart's place, where he left a name that will be fragrant forever. Alexander Duff was baptized for his dear friend.

And, brethren, this is a baptism that lies fresh upon us all today, at this Hallowtide. It lies upon us politically. You recall Lincoln's classic at Gettysburg. He said: "We cannot dedicate, we cannot consecrate, we cannot hallow this ground. The brave men . . . who struggled here have consecrated it far above our power to add or detract. . . . [Let us] here highly resolve that these dead shall not have died in vain." You could not get a better exposition of the great truth enshrined in our text. And then more recently in the Great World War, through the sacrifice and service of these years the same baptism was administered upon us. You remember how our young men went out. "Never again" was one of their slogans. A warless world! That is what that tablet there is saying to us today, on the eve of Armistice Day. That is what this recent baptism for the dead lays upon us as a holy trust.

> To you from failing hands, we throw
> The torch; be yours to hold it high.
> If ye break faith with us who die
> We shall not sleep, though poppies grow
> In Flanders Fields.

And religiously, too, there is a baptism that lies upon us. In John Bunyan's *Pilgrim's Progress,*

Greatheart on one occasion says to Gaius: "This woman is the wife of one, Christian, a pilgrim of former times, and these are his four children. And the boys all take after their father, and covet to tread in his steps. Yea, if they do see any print of his foot, it ministereth joy to their hearts and they covet to tread in the same." These boys were baptized for the dead in religious measures. And so it is with us today. There are the footprints which the pilgrims of old have left. We are challenged by a father's faith, a mother's piety, by all the splendid heroism and noble self-sacrifice and beautiful devotion of those who have gone before. We are dared by the graves of our sires to be baptized for the dead. And he is a poor and pitiable creature who will not accept the dare.

There is a story told in the life of Wendell Phillips. He and a young friend had been sitting by the fire for a whole evening. Memory had flushed the cheeks of the veteran abolitionist; the heroic days of the long ago came rushing back upon him; his tongue was unloosed and the old man completely lost himself in the thrilling recital. The youth sat enthralled. At last he realized that the evening was gone. And he rose to leave. As he took the old man's hand, he said, "Mr. Phillips, if I had lived in your time, I think I should have been heroic, too." And the veteran was aroused, and replied: "Young man, you are living in my time, and in God's time. And be sure of this: no man could have been heroic then, who is not heroic now. Good night." So it is. We are still living in heroic times. "Others have labored, and we have entered into their labors." "Baptized for the dead."

*Then one more Hallowtide truth, and that is that our debt to the past calls for payment in the present.* And we are indeed debtors. Think of our everyday conveniences of life. I shall not attempt to enumerate them. Or take our political heritage. You know the thrilling story of American institutions from the days of the Pilgrim Fathers down through the centuries since. And greatest of all was the creative force behind them all, that is, religion itself. You go back to Calvary. Our salvation itself was won at a great price. We are redeemed, not with corruptible things, as silver and gold, but with the precious blood of Christ. And so it is. Science, government and religion, all of them make us debtors. We are reaping where we have not sown. Indeed all that we have and all that we are, the things that are most precious and make life worth living, have come down to us through the toil and struggle and sacrifice of the ages. And it calls for some payment on our part.

Of course there are debts that we can never square. James Nasmyth, the inventor of the steam hammer, has told us in his autobiography the scenes that he used to witness as a boy in the old fish market in Edinburgh. He tells that after a wild and stormy night, when the husbands and sons had toiled at the risk of their lives to catch the fish, an intending buyer asked the usual question of a fishwife. "Weel, Janet, an hoo's the haddies the day?" And the fishwife replied meaningly: "Haddies? Haddies are men's lives the day." And yet the shining fish were sold for a few coppers. That did not pay for them. Robert Louis Stevenson in one of his essays says: "How little we pay our way in life! Although we have our purses continually in our hand, the better part of service still goes unrewarded." And what is true of fish, and many other articles of food and comfort, is also true of other spheres of human good. But though that be so, there is no mean measure of payment which we can all make, especially in the things of moral and spiritual value. The old Prussian, Frederick William, once said to his son, "If you lose what I've won, I'll laugh at you out of my grave." And I like that story of one of England's greatest statesmen. He often went into the old family portrait gallery. He stood as if in worship before the portraits, and he could be heard to say again and again: "I will not forget. I will be true." One day he took his eldest son with him, and he said to him, "My boy, you must hear these people speak." "But, father," said the lad, "what can they say?" Then his father, pointing to each portrait, said: "This one says, Be true to me. That one says, Be true to thyself. That other one says, Be true to your home. And that last one, which is my mother, says, Be true to God. And my son, I go out from them saying I will be true." And, brethren, that is the payment we can all make in the present, for our debt to the past. Whatever be our patrimony, whatever be the good which those who have gone before have enriched or blessed our life with, we are stewards. And "it is required in a steward that he be found faithful." The truth is that unless we give back to the world something that costs us blood and agony, we shall have failed and failed miserably and shamefully to discharge our just and honorable debt. During his Egyptian campaign Napoleon pointed to the Pyramids and cried, "Soldiers, forty centuries look down upon you." And so it is. "What shall they do which are baptized for the dead?"

I have a tryst to keep
With those who lie asleep.

# MORNING VISIONS

One of the most rewarding books of the season is *The Autobiography of a Mind,* by Dr. Dawson, in which we learn more about him than facts and dates can tell us. It is a book of beauty and wisdom, the story of a poet, a mystic, a seerlike mind, its visions and visitations, its moods and memories, recalled in mellow, meditative years, in a style limpid and lovely—like an old violin which remembers all the melodies it has heard. No one can forget the chapter entitled "My Mother," and surely no preacher can read the last chapter but one without being strangely subdued.

A son of the parsonage, "old style," Dr. Dawson was born in Northamptonshire, "the forty-ninth State of the Union," as befitted a man who was to spend many years in America. After three great pastorates, two in London and the other in Glasgow, he came to America in 1905, settling as minister of the Old First Church of Newark; from which he recently resigned—retiring from the active ministry at the age of seventy-one, giving us as a benediction his autobiography and a new edition of *The Man Christ Jesus,* the writing of which took him to the Holy Land, in which he found the Fifth Gospel.

Out of a long row of books by Dr. Dawson, most of which it has been my joy to read, those most vividly remembered are *The House of Dreams,* where the mystic dwells; *The Forgotten Secret,* a jewel in the literature of prayer; and the best picture known to me of church life in New York City, *A Prophet in Babylon,* to which must be added his life of Jesus. It means much to have lived so fruitful a life, and to come to the end of his ministry with a heart full of Morning Visions.

# MORNING VISIONS

W. J. DAWSON, D.D.

OLD FIRST CHURCH, NEWARK

*In the morning will I direct my prayer unto Thee, and will look up.* Psalm 5: 3.

The upward look, that is what I wish to talk of to you this morning. When you wake in the morning, look up. The sun is put in the heaven for you, and it is ingratitude not to lift your eyes to his beams. When you pray, look up; a great deal of prayer fails for want of the upward look. As you go about this life, learn to look up; the best things are all above you, the sky, the green boughs and the traveling clouds. "I will lift up mine eyes unto the hills," said the Psalmist in another place; that man lives only a poor low life who cannot see the distant and the high. There are blue distances in life; train your eyes to see them. Life cannot be lived well without upward thought; it is only the beast that keeps its head down, and that is because its life is a browsing life. The upward look—why, it is that which makes man noble; it is the mark of his kinship with the eternities, without it he is even as the beasts. Here then is plenty for us to think of for half an hour, a whole treasury of wisdom packed away into this brief phrase, "I will look up."

In the morning I will look up, says the Psalmist. Have you noticed that a great deal in the character of the day depends on the direction given to it in its earliest hours, on its first word, thought, act, and emotion? The first moment of the day is a tuning fork and you strike the keynote of the whole day with it. Flowers give forth their strongest perfume in the morning hours, and so do thoughts. Our first thought when we wake gives perfume to the day. All those who have written or spoken on the art of life know this. Most of us rise too hastily; enter on the toil of the day too precipitately; and the result is a hurried, feverish mode of living, which wears out heart and nerve by misdirected energy. We have all sorts of remedies today for tired hearts and broken nerves, but the best and most accessible of all remedies is acquaintance with the peace of God. One hour of quiet fellowship with God in the early morning, one deep draught of God's tranquillity before the heat and burden of the day begin, will do more for us than all the doctors, and all the medicines. No wiser thing, be sure of it, was ever said upon the art of living, than this saying of the Shepherd Psalmist, "In the morning I will look up."

I lived in a part of London known as Islington for twelve years, and as I walked the thronged streets I sometimes thought of the days when they were green fields, and of a man who has left an imperishable mark on English literature who moved across them: old Izaak Walton, the author of *The Compleat Angler*. There is a morning freshness in his writings, a charm of dew and early sunshine and heartfelt felicity. Listen to his morning meditation:

> There are many men [he writes] that are of others taken to be serious grave men, which we condemn and pity; men of sour complexions, money-getting men, that spend all their time first in getting and next in anxious care of it; men that are condemned to be rich and always discontented and busy. For these poor rich men we pity them, and stand in no need to borrow their thoughts to think ourselves happy, for we enjoy a contentedness above the reach of such dispositions.

That was a morning meditation; one feels the dew of heaven fresh upon it. "Poor rich men, condemned to be rich"—it needs the enfranchisement of a fresh May morning to make one feel and speak like this. "Give me health and a day, and I will make the pomp of empire ridiculous," said Emerson; and so felt this old fisherman as he walked in the sweet loneliness of a May morning, drinking in the peace of God. Here, assuredly, was a man who knew what it meant to direct his prayer to God in the morning and look up.

The wise words of Izaak Walton suggest to me a personal experience. On one of my walking tours in Switzerland many years ago I found myself one morning in the little valley of Stalden, on the road to Zermatt. It was five o'clock, the mists were lifting from the mountains, and already the greater heights were bathed in sunshine. From the tower of the village church a bell rang, and across the pastures moved long files of peasant-folk going to early mass. All that day this morning picture lingered with me, and I felt in it a gracious suggestion of something sacred and holy in human life. Did not the sweet memory of that morning hour linger also with these humble worshipers through all the hard toil of the day? Was it not a noble beginning of a day, which filled all its hours with the divine perfume of quiet thoughts and heavenly aspirations?

There are days in our lives which seem wholly discordant. Have we ever tried to discover the cause of this discord? You all recognize the kind of day I mean. It is the day when everything goes wrong, when we lose our tempers on small provocations, when we are worried to madness by little things—mere pin pricks and scratches, which would be normally disregarded, but become smarting sores and inflamed wounds. Well, what was wrong? Was it not that we began wrong? We sought no sacred altar when we woke and had no sacrifice of gratitude to bring to it. We never so much as lifted our eyes to the morning heavens in thankfulness for the light and praise for the mercy of sleep. We struck the wrong note in our first waking moment, and it vibrated through the whole day. In the morning we did not look up and direct our prayer to God.

The upward look—there are many names for it. Its first name is prayer: in the morning I will look up and *direct my prayer* to Thee. I have already said that there is a kind of prayer which is not looking up, but looking down; and there is small help, but rather great injury in this kind of prayer. It is prayer which is concerned entirely with our own affairs. In a history of Wessex which I once read there is recorded a quaint prayer of this kind, uttered by a man named John Ward, who lived in 1727. This was his prayer: "O Lord, I beseech Thee to have an eye of compassion on the County of Hertfordshire, for I have a mortgage in that County. Likewise give, I beseech Thee, a prosperous voyage to the *Mermaid* sloop, because I have not insured it." Now that is not prayer at all, it is merely an attempt to make God a partner in a commercial transaction. It is true that we are told *in everything* by prayer and supplication to make our requests known unto God, but surely a man comes unworthily before God, who has nothing better to talk about than his loans and mortgages, and mercantile adventures. That was Jacob's idea of God, when he received from Isaac the blessing, "God give thee of the dew of heaven, and the fatness of the earth, and plenty of corn and wine." But there came an hour, when the awfulness of God was revealed to him, when he saw in a dream the angel-crowded ladder between earth and heaven, and after that he prayed not for the fatness of the earth, but that God would give him bread only and bring him to his father's house in peace. He was looking upward now, not downward. A sweet and sacred fear possessed him, he was afraid and said "How dreadful is this place! this is none other but the house of God, and this is the gate of heaven."

And this also was our Lord's conception of prayer, abundantly manifest in the prayer which specially bears His name, and has been for ages the model of all prayer. For if you examine the Lord's Prayer, what do you find? But a single petition which has to do with man's physical existence: "Give us this day our daily bread." Petition for personal good is in every other case petition for spiritual good, the forgiveness of offenses, the conquest of temptation, the deliverance from evil, and all the rest is ascription, aspiration, and consecration to the Will of God. This is the prayer which looks up and finds the heaven opened.

> The opening heavens around me shine
> With beams of sacred bliss
> When Jesus shows His mercy mine
> And whispers I am His.

For true prayer is not an effort to enlist the will of God on the side of our desires, but to bring our desires into conformity to the will of God. It is the desire to find the harmony of our life in the will of God; and when the end of life came for Jesus there was only one clause of his own immortal prayer which lingered on His lips, "Thy will, not mine, be done."

Here is the prayer that looks up and is the ladder on which the many-splendored shapes of holiness and beauty move. All other prayer, being fixed upon the earth, sees only the sad and perplexing visions of the earth.

The upward look: another name for it is aspiration. Most of the evil in human life comes from looking down. Our dejections, our dismays, our melancholies—what are they but the fruit of looking down? There is always daylight in the fields of space, but only they see it whose eyes look up. And is not one source of our sins also the downward look? David walked on the palace roof and looked down; had his eyes been lifted to the eternal purities above him, how different had been his story! He looked down, and in that moment he began to go down. He looked down to the carnalities of earth, and straightway entered on that long and shameful path which led to adultery and murder. There are some of us who know the kind of ruin wrought by the downward look. But when we confess that our lives are bemired with evil, let us also remember that as the downward look brought us into the mire, so the first step in getting out of the mire is the upward look. The aspiration for better things is the first element in redemption from evil things. Lift up your thought; don't grovel, don't be ignominiously content with your defilement. Learn to say, as a very dubious hero in one of Oscar Wilde's plays says, "We are all in the gutter, but some of us are looking at the stars." Evil is never irretrievable as long as we have the grace to recognize the stars of faith and purity.

Rossetti has a beautiful picture of Mary Magdalene at the door of Simon the Pharisee, and has written a yet more beautiful sonnet on the same scene, in which he makes all the gracious change in the woman who was a sinner begin with an upward look. She is passing with her earthly lover intent only on fading joys, when she is arrested by the beauty and purity of the face of Jesus and she cries:

"O loose me—seest thou not my Bridegroom's face,
That draws me to Him? For His feet my kiss—
My hair, my tears, He craves today; and, Oh,
What words can tell what other day and place
Shall see me clasp those blood-stained feet of His?
He needs me—calls me—loves me: let me go."

She looked up, and that was the beginning of her redemption. She saw eternal love, and all other love of ardent flesh and tingling pulses became worthless. A new aspiration after spiritual beauty was born in her at that moment, and a new life began. And it is so with us, who have looked down so long—"There is life for a look at the Crucified One. There is life at this moment for thee."

The upward look: A third name for it is Courage. Whatever the defeats and misfortunes of yesterday, there is always a new birth of courage in the dawn of a new day. When we look upon the spaciousness and tranquillity of a morning sky, the specters of fear and grief which haunted the night are forgotten. Recently millions of eyes looked up to the great wonder of the heavens, where gigantic and almost immeasurable processes were at work, and what was our dominant thought? Mine was, the eternal steadfastness of the starry order. Things go wrong in the human world, but they never go wrong there. Timed to a moment the great shadow falls upon the earth, and at a sudden predestined moment the light returns. If ever there was an occasion to say "God's in His heaven, all's right with the world," this was the occasion.

And to think this is to be of good courage, it is to face the problems of human life with a new fortitude and serenity of temper. Looking down, walking with our eyes fixed only on an earth often veiled in strange shadows, we lose courage. But, looking up, we perceive God at work, eternal strength and wisdom engaged in an eternal Task, and we learn to say:

"High in the heavens, eternal God,
Thy goodness in full glory shines.
Thy truth shall break through every cloud
That veils and darkens Thy designs."

And it seems to me that what we most need in the life of our own day is this note of cheerful courage. So many of our leaders, thinkers, and writers, have lost the upward look; all their looks are downward, and so they are destitute of the spirit of genial courage. Thomas Hardy, who is accounted one of the chief priests of modern pessimism, has himself explained its origin, when he speaks of "The melancholy which has overwhelmed the civilized peoples of today with the decline of belief in God." When the belief in God departs, belief in life also perishes. Its gravity and splendor are not discerned, only its paltriness and misery. What wonder that genial courage deserts us? We see it even in our modern humor. How acrid much of it is, how spiteful and ill-natured! How different from the robust mirth-compelling humor of Charles Dickens, for example! And the difference is that Dickens, with all his knowledge of the darker side of life by bitter experience, nevertheless believed in life. He was not afraid to look down into the abyss of human suffering, but he always saw the rainbow above the abyss, the sacred fidelities and affections which gave a divine quality to the humblest existence. Be sure of this, no man can be a true helper of his fellows who has only downward looks, always quick to discover the sordidness and meanness of human life, but averse from the vision of its inherent beauties.

And yet another name for the upward look is Hope. For Courage is the Child of Hope. Perhaps you will recall the great picture of Hope by Watts, known to millions by endless reproduction: and if you do, you will remember that at first sight it appears much more a picture of Despair than Hope. The figure he paints is of a woman seated on a dark globe in what appears the last abandonment of dejection. Her head is bowed and her eyes are sightless. In her hand is a lyre, all the strings of which are broken, save one—and that one string is Hope. It is the symbol of "something in man, which is always on the eve of disappearing, but never disappears: an assurance which is always apparently saying farewell, but yet illimitably lingers: a string which is always stretched to snapping, and yet never breaks."

Hope, that is the whole message of Christianity. Hope in God, hope in yourself, hope for your brother man. "The God of Hope" is one of the most beautiful descriptions of God found in the Bible. In spite of the age-long apostasies and errors of men, God is still hopeful of His children, and bids them hope. That one string is never silenced, and I think it is never so audible as in the morning hours when out of the depths of night day returns newborn in perpetual resurrection. In the morning, then, I will look up; for there is one thing about the morning which we have all felt: it creates in us the sense of a new chance.

Here hath been dawning
Another blue day,
Think, wilt thou let it
Slip useless away?

## W. J. Dawson, D.D.

Our yesterdays discourage us, our todays quicken us to new endeavor. No man has ever looked upon a daybreak without some inarticulate sense of new-born opportunity. It is in the night that ghosts walk, the specters of old doubts and sorrows, but at the first breath of morning they depart. The rising sun is a golden trumpet on which God summons the host of mankind to forget the things which are behind and to press on to the things which are before. After the dark struggle by the brook, full of mystery and pain, the sun rises on Jacob, and he sees his life opening out before him in an infinite wealth of promise. "And when the morning was now come, Jesus stood on the shore," writes the Evangelist, and it is as though he said: "It is always dark till Jesus appears, but when He comes, He brings the morning with Him." It was an Easter morning when He rose, and the first thing His eyes, opening out of death, beheld, was a fair garden, calm and lovely in the early sun-light. For the sun was no longer darkened; Calvary and all its terror was forgotten; He came back to a world of daylight, where the dawn made all things new.

Once more God gives us a day—a Sabbath day. Let us on this sacred morning direct our prayer to God and look up, going out to the work and conflict of our daily life with new courage because we have communed with Him who is Light, and have received into our hearts the cheerful messages of Day. And from the high towers of Dawn, as from the muezzin towers of oriental cities, a voice of challenge and of Hope salutes us:

> "Awake, thou that sleepest,
> Arise from the dead, and
> Christ shall give thee Light."

THE END